D1559675

Jackie Mitchell:
The Girl Who Loved
Baseball

By John M. Kovach

WALDENHOUSE PUBLISHERS, INC.
WALDEN, TENNESSEE

Jackie Mitchell: The Girl Who Loved Baseball

Published by Waldenhouse Publishers, Inc.
100 Clegg Street, Signal Mountain, Tennessee 37377 USA
423-886-2721   www.waldenhouse.com
Printed in the United States of America
Type and Design by Karen Paul Stone

About the cover: Wearing a Signal School For Girls sweater, Jackie Mitchell jumps to catch a line drive. c.1930. Source:*Diamond Dreams Collection*

ISBN: 978-1-947589-40-7 Case Binding (hard cover)
ISBN: 978-1-947589-41-4 Perfect Binding (soft cover)
Library of Congress Control Number: 2021939967
Describes the professional baseball career of female pitcher Jackie Mitchell through newspaper accounts, including her 1931 strikeouts of Babe Ruth and Lou Gehrig. Includes 16 season statistical charts along with some never seen before images among the 23 photographs and illustrations. -- provided by Publisher
BIO016000 BIOGRAPHY AND AUTOBIOGRAPHY/ Sports
SPO003030 SPORTS & RECREATION / Baseball / History
SPO003040 SPORTS & RECREATION / Baseball / Statistics

Dedication

For all of the girls like Jackie who love baseball and want to follow their dreams of playing in the major leagues

Table Of Contents

Illustrations

Acknowledgments

Over a three-year time period, many people have been instrumental with bringing the elements of Jackie Mitchell's baseball story together. At the top of that list is the welcoming staff from the Local History Department at the Chattanooga Public Library. When in person research slowed due to COVID-19, the staff helped to continue to answer questions via email. I especially want to note the patience of Suzette Raney, Archivist in Local History and Genealogy at the Chattanooga Public Library.

Researching women's baseball over the years, I have those favorite go-to folks to either share information, theories or just to work through elements of a story. In that regard, fellow researchers Barbara Gregorich, author of *Women At Play* and Dr. Debra A. Shattuck, *Bloomer Girls: Women Baseball Pioneers* are at the top of my list.

My list would not be complete without including Kevin Wadzinski of the St. Joseph County (Indiana) Public Library for his willingness to hunt through early *Chattanooga City Directories*. I also want to thank Chattanooga author David Jenkins for sharing his memories of an interview he conducted with Jackie in the early 1980s.

I would also like to thank Jackie's nephew, Spencer Mitchell Melton. He was patient with my questions about possible family ties to Memphis, Tennessee and was happy that people were, "still talking about my Aunt Jackie."

A very special thank you to Waldenhouse editor and publisher, Karen Paul Stone for her patience, guidance and direction in helping to bring Jackie's story to a new audience.

Finally, a special thanks to all of the libraries, big and small, who often went above and beyond to look in their local publications for anything about Jackie Mitchell.

Introduction

Fans of baseball history love stories. Over the course of time however, aspects of a story begin to blur and some of the facts may become slightly altered. Spread the re-telling out over three or four generations and the changed story suddenly become THE story.

This is the conundrum for a researcher of history.

In 2016, while preparing for a talk about the history of girls and women in baseball in my new hometown of Memphis, Tennessee, I wanted to bring a local "hook" to the talk.

As I poured through scans of old news articles and notes from previous talks, I came up with two possibilities. One had a relatively recent tie to Memphis, the other was from Chattanooga, Tennessee. One option would be the story of Molly McKesson. In the mid-2000's, McKesson, a young female baseball player from Florida became the first female scholarship baseball player to play at the NCAA, Division II level when she signed with Christian Brothers University in Memphis.

My second choice was Virne Beatrice Mitchell. Most of the baseball world knew her as Jackie Mitchell. In 1931, she signed a professional baseball contract with the Chattanooga Lookouts and struck out Babe Ruth and Lou Gehrig in a preseason exhibition game. I was strongly leaning toward the McKesson story. However, that changed after reading a 1931 article that said as a young girl, Mitchell lived and played sandlot baseball in Memphis AND was taught how to pitch by Baseball Hall of Famer, Arthur "Dazzy" Vance of the Memphis Chicks. The Chicks were members of the Southern Association, a minor league circuit.

I was familiar with Mitchell's story------or at least I thought I was. The basic story line was that Mitchell was 17 years old in April of 1931 when she struck out Ruth and Gehrig. Afterwards, Baseball Commissioner Kenesaw Mountain Landis voided her contract on the basis that baseball was too strenuous for females. Voiding her contract left Mitchell to play in outlaw leagues and barnstorm with teams including the House of David.

Previous books about Mitchell spend the majority of their text detailing and analyzing the two-thirds of an inning from an April exhibition game in 1931. Interviews with Mitchell from that time show that she was a young woman with a strong love of baseball. Few books however, spend time talking about what she did before (or after) that day. A female baseball pitcher, with ties to a Hall of Fame baseball pitcher in the late 1920s and early 1930s is going to be news, especially in her hometown. This was the Mitchell I wanted to know more about.

The only mention of Jackie playing baseball as a young girl was from a 1933 feature article on February 12 in the *Chattanooga Daily News*. Reporter Jubeth Gorman recounted a story told by Jackie's mother, Virne.

The story was from the summer of 1923, when Jackie was nine years old. She had just come home for lunch after playing baseball with the little boys in her neighborhood. When Jackie talked about going back out to play again after lunch, her mother disapproved of her playing with the boys, said, "Now you may well realize, you are not going to play ball with those boys this afternoon."

Jackie's reply was, "Well, all right. But they will be a man short if I don't play."

With few hard facts in hand, thus began my search for Jackie Mitchell – the girl who loved baseball.

CHAPTER 1
Memphis and Dazzy Vance

The first mention of a Mitchell family connection to Memphis was on March 22, 1931, newspaper story following Jackie's attendance at a baseball camp in Atlanta. However, in April of that same year, the story was repeated in news articles prior to and just after Jackie's pitching appearance against the Yankees and became more widespread.

Most of the articles state the Mitchell family had lived in Memphis about 10 years prior to Jackie's appearance with the Lookouts. There are numerous variations of the "facts" as well as the time period in the Mitchell-Vance connection. Some accounts say that Jackie is between the ages of 5-9 and that the Mitchell family either lives on the same block, same duplex, same house or next door to Memphis Chicks pitcher Dazzy Vance.

This same story is told in *Dazzy Vance: A Biography of the Brooklyn Dodgers Hall of Famer* written by John C. Skip-

Brooklyn Dodgers pitcher and baseball Hall of Famer Dazzy Vance. When pitching for the Memphis Chicks in 1917-18, Vance reportedly lived near the Mitchell family and taught a young lefthanded Jackie to throw a baseball. (Source: Diamond Dreams Collection)

per in 2007. One chapter mentions the Mitchell-Vance connection, citing the July 23, 1933 *New York Times,* column, "Here And There In Sports", by Bryan Field. The column mentioned that the two families lived in adjoining apartments "13 years ago" and that Vance took an interest in six year old Jackie "because she was a lefthander and could throw straight and far."

Vance was a member of the Chicks for a number of seasons, having played for them in 1917, 1918 and again in 1920. Vance joined the Chicks on July 10, 1917 and is with the team until June 30, 1918 when he becomes a member of the New York Yankees. This would also place Jackie's age in Memphis between five and six years of age. Possibly the right age to be taught to pitch by a Hall of Famer. Definitely not of the right age to have played sandlot baseball in Memphis.

Two other records that verify Vance's tie to Memphis would be for the birth (September, 1918) and death (October, 1920) for his son Donald..

In 1919, Vance is playing minor league baseball in Sacramento, California and then in 1920, he splits time between Memphis and New Orleans. Although there are a number of Arthur Vance's living in Memphis between 1917-21, only the 1921 Memphis city directory can he be identified for sure. In that directory he is listed as "Dazzy Vance, Ballplayer", boarding at 1015 Rayburn Blvd.

The next search was to locate the Mitchell family in Memphis.

The Mitchell family had longtime ties to Chattanooga, Tennessee. The April, 1931 newspaper articles named Jackie's father as Joseph S. Mitchell, respected optician in Chattanooga. His obituary in 1949 stated that Mitchell had been in the optometry business in Chattanooga for over 30 years. It also mentioned that as a young man, he went to Mississippi, but returned to Chattanooga about 1910 to open his business. Among his survivors, was a young grandchild by the name of Spencer Mitchell Melton, living in Miami, Florida.

According to Hamilton County, Tennessee records, Joseph S. Mitchell married Virne Wall on December 23, 1911. Over the next few years in Hamilton County would come of the births of daughters Virne Beatrice (Jackie) on August 29, 1912 and Josephine Nora on December 27, 1914. Looking at those birth records, Jackie could not have been 17 in 1931 when she struck out Ruth and Gehrig. Her actual age would have been 18 (closer to 19) in April of 1931.

This is a copy of the August 29, 1912, Hamilton County Tennessee Birth record for Verne Beatrice (Jackie) Mitchell. Based on this record, Jackie Mitchell was 18 years of age (almost 19) when she struck out Babe Ruth and Lou Gehrig on April 2, 1931. Original newspaper reports from her signing a contract with the Chattanooga Lookouts and game appearance against the New York Yankees gave her age as 17. (Source: Ancestry.com)

This would be the first of a number of instances where the story of Jackie would change. Jackie's age aside however, it was important to locate the Mitchell family in Chattanooga to develop the timeline of when the family lived in Memphis.

Joseph S. Mitchell was born in the town of Sparta in Wright County, Tennessee in October of 1890. The 1900 census would show his family living in the town of Guntersville, Alabama. In that census, Joseph is nine years old.

In 1911, Mitchell would marry his wife Virne and they would be listed in the *Chattanooga City Directory* up through 1914. Joseph is working in various capacities for the Walsh & Weidner Boiler Company. Between 1915-1918, Joseph would disappear from the *Chattanooga City Directory* listings.

Based on Joseph Mitchell's date of birth, there was another record from the 1914-18 time period that did locate the Mitchell family. Joseph would have filled out a World War I draft card. It would list his place of birth, age, residence and occupation.

Mitchell's draft card was found in an unexpected place. On June 5, 1917, Joseph S. Mitchell filled out his card in the city of Enid, Garfield County, Oklahoma. It is the correct Joseph S. Mitchell. His card states that he is married with two children; was born on October 31, 1890 in Sparta, Wright County, Tennessee and he is working at the Bon-Eye Optical Com-

The June 5, 1917, World War I draft card record for Jackie Mitchell's father, Joseph S. Mitchell. This record is the first one to show Mr. Mitchell working in the optometry business, an occupation he would become well-known for after the family moved to Chattanooga in 1919. (Source: Familysearch.org)

pany. This is also the first record of his working in the optometry business. Joseph Mitchell's 1949 obituary mentions he spent time in Mississippi, but does not specify a city or town. A 1933 *New York Times* feature article about Jackie, mentions her dad, Joseph, played in the Cotton States League, "20 years ago." Although there were a number of Mississippi teams in the Cotton States League, there are no minor league records indicating that a Joseph/Joe Mitchell played in the league between 1902-1913.

In May of 2017, I spoke to Spencer Melton, Jackie's nephew and her closest living relative at his home in Miami. Spencer's mother was the only child of Josephine and her husband Spencer Melton. Mr. Melton who was born in 1949, was somewhat surprised to get a call regarding his aunt and was happy to know that people still thought about her. However, when queried about any family connection to Memphis, he did not have anything to share. He said that he never recalled his mother talking about Memphis, nor as a child, he could not remember ever visiting there.

In the *Memphis City Directory* listing between 1914 and 1918, there are a number of Jos./Joe/Joseph's listed, including a Joseph S. in 1917. However, there is no indication in either the alphabetical listings or business listing under "Opticians" for a Mitchell. And, even with those Mitchell's listed in that time period, none are living near anyone named Vance.

Of all of the Mitchells listed in Memphis between 1914-18, there is one of interest. In 1918, there is a John S. Mitchell, whose occupation is that of an optician. He works at the Washburn-Lyle Drug Store and boards at 267 S. Main St. This is the only city directory that lists a Mitchell as an optician in Memphis in the 1914-18 time period. And, just as in the case of the Joseph Mitchell listings, there is not anyone named Vance living close by.

Is John S. really Joseph S.? It would fit the timeline as to when Vance was pitching for the Chicks. However, not finding Mitchell and Vance in close living proximity would seem to cast doubt on the story of Jackie's time in Memphis.

Finally, it was time to check the *Memphis Commercial Appeal* newspaper for clarification of the Mitchell-Vance connection. Between March 22 and April 12, 1931, there are no less than six articles about Jackie in the paper. Not one of them mentions the fact that she may have lived in Memphis as a young girl and there were no mentions of the connection between her and former Memphis Chicks pitcher Dazzy Vance.

Some articles were wire stories that also appeared in other newspapers. Interestingly, almost every one of the non-Memphis papers mentioned her connection to the city and Vance while the local paper did not. One would have thought for sure, a local beat writer, seeing a wire story mentioning the connection would have dug into the possibility. For whatever reason, that was not done.

So, based on all of the available information and the lack of living witnesses, it's possible that the 1918 city directory listing of John S. Mitchell, was a mistake and the 1917-18 time slot is the only one that would make sense for Mitchell and Vance to have connected in Memphis. It is also possible that both Mitchell and Vance may have arrived in town after one city directory had been canvassed and left before the next one was undertaken.

However, in August of 1919, the *Chattanooga Daily Times* confirmed that the Mitchell family did indeed come to town from Memphis. The August 2 story was headlined, "J.S. Mitchell Purchases H.W. Johnson Business." The article noted that Mitchell, "recently of Memphis has purchased the stock and good will of H. W. Johnson, and will continue the optical business at the old stand on East Eighth Street."

CHAPTER 2
The Engelettes

It may well go done in history as the first-ever all girls baseball league, as the headline in the April 26, 1930, *Chattanooga Daily Times* read: "Girls' Baseball Loop Formed By Four Clubs."

The article noted that the four teams comprising the Girls' City Baseball League were the Peerless Woolen Mills, Soddy Hosiery Mills, the Dixie Spinning Mills of Lupton City and the Engelettes. Managers for each club were also named. Soddy would be headed by Campbell; Moore would manage Dixie while Garnett McMillan coached Peerless and Arch McDonald led the Engelettes.

A league constitution was adopted on April 25, and rules for the league would be the same as those used by the City, Interstate and Industrial League for boys. The rosters would be limited to 18 players, and the player contracts would need to be filed with the league secretary by 6 p.m. on May 8.

A few days before the season opened, the league was reorganized. It would still be a four-team circuit, however Richmond Hosiery Mills, managed by Woods would replace Dixie Spinning Mills.

League president Chester Holmes and secretary Buddy Martin announced that the league would play a 15 game schedule and would include some tilts to be played at Engel Stadium before Lookout games or on days the minor league team was out of town. They also added that Gordon Gambill and Ed Ricketts would serves as umpires for the league.

The May 10 league opener would pit the Soddy Hosiery Mills against Peerless Hosiery Mills at Warner Park, followed by the May 11 contest between Richmond and the Engelettes at Engel Stadium. That game would

Aucassin and Nicolete

(A Dramatized Song-Story)

Given by

SIGNAL SCHOOL FOR GIRLS

May 20th, 8 O'Clock, Warner Park

SYNOPSIS OF PLAY

The story is laid in Provence, France, in the thirteenth century. Aucassin, son of Count Garin de Beaucaire falls in love with Nicolete, a captive maid. His father, very displeased, makes a covenant with him that if he will go out and defend his country against Count Bougais de Valence, who is besieging the city, that he will allow him to see Nicolete, who is imprisoned. Aucassin fights successfully, but his father refuses to keep his vow and has his son imprisoned. Nicolete, in the meanwhile, slips from her prison and goes to bid Aucassin farewell before she goes to hide in the forest. As soon as Aucassin is freed, he goes to seek Nicolete. After a long search he finds her, but as they start away together, Paynim bandits seize Nicolete and leave Aucassin unconscious. For years he wanders, during which time his father dies. At last he returns to his own city. There Nicolete, disguised as a minstrel, sings him her story, and finally the two are united.

SCENES

I. The Castle of Beaucaire.
II. The Castle of Beaucaire.
III. The Battlefield.
IV. Outside a dungeon of Beaucaire.
V. The Forest.
VI. The Forest.
VII. The Castle of Beaucaire.

CHARACTERS

(In order of their appearance)

The Jogleur..Sara Marr
His Lad...Lucretia Carl
Page..Beatrice Mitchell
Garin de Beaucaire..................................Frances Cleage
Captain of City....................................Virginia Reeves
Aucassin..Anna Peglar
Nicolete..Miriam Carter
Lords and Ladies—Marjorie Carter, Dorothy Poste, Dorothy Browder, Willie Kittrell, Adelaide Beck, Evelyn Dixon, Elizabeth Bryan, Ruth Acree, Mary Hellman, Jean Ferguson, Minnie Grindler, Jessie Mae Faris, Mary B. Duncan.
Two Soldiers of Beaucaire............Billy Annis, Elizabeth Hellman
Two Soldiers of Valence..............Carolyn McNabb, Evelyn Dixon
Count Boregais de Valence.............................Mary Goss
Sentinel..Aileen Cochran
Shepherds—Dorothy Wenning, Carolyn Rape, Sara Sue Robinson, Madeline Dawn.
A Lady of the Court...............................Josephine Smith
Councillor..Ruth Goss
Gypsies....Carolyn McNabb, Christine Gray, Kate Ferrell, Margie Cleage

Between 1928 and 1930, Beatrice (Jackie) Mitchell attended the Signal School For Girls. During that time she appeared in at least two school plays. This is a copy of a program from the Aucassin and Nicolette play in which Beatrice (Jackie) played the part of a Page. The play took place on May 20, 1927 at Warner Park in Chattanooga. (Source: Signal School For Girls Scrapbook, 1925-30, Chattanooga Public Library Collection)

mark the first time in baseball history that a girls baseball game would be played prior to the start of a professional men's baseball contest.

Of the four teams, the Engelettes appeared to have a tie to Joe Engel, owner of the Chattanooga Lookouts minor league team. The team may have been sponsored by Engel. Another link to Engel and the Lookouts was Arch McDonald, the girls team manager. He served as the Lookouts radio broadcaster.

The day before the Engelettes opened their season, a team photograph was published in the *Chattanooga News,* referring to the team as "Joe Engel and His Engelettes."

Cast photograph from the Signal School For Girls play, Aucassin and Nicolette.
Beatrice (Jackie) Mitchell is in the back row, third from the left. (Source: Signal
School For Girls Scrapbook, 1925-30, Chattanooga Public Library Collection)

Pictured with Engel were 10 team members including Bill Wetzel who
has recently won the Southeastern A.A.U. (Amateur Athletic Union) Baseball Throw in Atlanta, Georgia. Of the eight players not pictured, the most
notable on the list was a lefthanded pitcher by the name of Beatrice Mitchell. Coming into that first season for the Girl's League, Mitchell would have
been a freshman at the Signal School For Girls or Chattanooga's Central
High School. She does not appear in the 1930 Central Yearbook, but her
younger sister Josephine is listed as a sophomore. There are no known cop-
ies of any Signal School For Girls yearbooks. The only known documenta-
tion for the school is a small scrapbook in the collection of the Chattanooga
Public Library. Jackie (listed as Beatrice) does appear a few times in that
scrapbook, but only as a participant in school plays.

Less than a year from her debut in the Girl's League, Mitchell would
bring national attention to the Chattanooga Lookouts.

The first time Mitchell (who would go by the first name of Jack in news accounts throughout the season) appears in a game result for the Engelettes is on June 8. At that time the Engelettes had a record of 2-1. She was the pitcher of record in the second game of a doubleheader played against Soddy Hosiery at Engel Stadium. Mitchell gave up six hits and 12 runs in pitching a complete game, 14-12 win.

ENGELETTES, SODDY SPLIT DOUBLE BILL

Visitors Take Opener, 24-6— Locals Come Through in Nightcap, 14-12.

Soddy and Engelettes split a double bill at Engel stadium yesterday, the first tilt going to the visitors, 24 to 6, the nightcap to the Engelettes, 14 to 12. N. Grant twirled both contests for the Soddy girls, giving up nine hits in the opener and seven in the second game.

E. Coleman and Varner hit homers with the bases full in the first game. Harvey secured a single, two triples and two doubles out of six times at bat to lead the stick work of the visitors, while Timmons hit well for the Engelettes.

In the second game Oyler and N. Grant, both of Soddy, and Timmons and McNabb, of the Engelettes, shone at bat. Scores:

FIRST GAME.

	R.	H.
Soddy Hosiery Mill	24	21
Engelettes	6	9

Batteries N. Grant and Harvey; Trumbull and Wetzel.
Umpire—Coughlan.

SECOND GAME.

	R.	H.
Soddy Hosiery Mill	13	6
Engelettes	14	7

Batteries—N. Grant and Harvey; Mitchell and Wetzel.
Umpire Coughlan.

This June 7, 1930 game is the first time that Jackie Mitchell can be documented playing baseball for an organized team, pitching a complete game, 14-12 win. Source: Chattanooga Daily Times, June 8, 1930, p.18)

On June 14, Mitchell went head to head against 13-year-old Elizabeth Brandon, another lefty in the league. Both pitchers would toss a complete game and strike out 10 batters. However, Mitchell ended up on the short end of a 20-6 score. It would mark the only time during the season that the two lefties faced each other.

The following week was also a struggle for Mitchell as she was knocked out early in a 25-9 loss to Richmond Hosiery. Reeling from those back to back losses, the Engelettes forfeited their next contest to Soddy Hosiery on June 28, leaving their record at 2-5.

Taking a break from league play, the Engelettes ventured to Cleveland, Tennessee on July 3 to take on a men's team from the Bacon Hosiery Mills. Although Mitchell did not start the game for the Engelettes, she hurled the last three innings, surrendering six runs and took the loss with an 11-7 final score. The game reports from both Cleveland and Chattanooga offered the first commentary regarding Mitchell's pitching skills as both local newspapers said that she had "good control."

Two days later, the Engelettes returned to league contests as they dropped an 18-5 loss to the Peerless Woolen Mills. On July 12, Mitchell was on the mound at Engel Stadium facing the Richmond Hosiery club. She was knocked out of the box and took the loss in a 19-8 final score.

With a record of 2-7, there was a managerial change for the Engelettes. Joe Mitchell (Jackie's father), took over the club reins for the July 19 game against the Soddy Hosiery Mills. The story was pretty much the same as the past few games as the Engelettes lost by a score of 29-4. Mitchell did not start the game. She was the third of three pitchers used that day. A week later, a 12-6 loss to Peerless found the Engelettes with a record of 2-9.

As the season entered its final stages, the Engelettes got back to the win column on August 2, with a 29-19 win over Richmond Hosiery. Mitchell for her part tossed a complete game, striking out 10 batters as well as walloping a double and a triple at the plate.

Mitchell was on the mound the next week against the Soddy Hosiery Mills team, hurling a complete game, but surrendering 17 hits and 17 runs in a 17-4 loss.

That weekend, Soddy Hosiery Mills laid claim to the league title with a final record of 11-3. Peerless Woolen Mills was second with a 9-5 mark, Richmond Hosiery took third place with their record of 4-9 while the Engelettes sat in fourth place at 3-10.

On August 16 in Cleveland, Tennessee, the Engelettes took on a picked team made up of members of the Richmond and Soddy Hosiery Mills girls league teams. The Engelettes defeated the picked team by a score of 14-13 behind the hitting of Mitchell, Wetzel and McNabb.

On August 22, the Engelettes would face a men's team for the second time that season. Facing the Woodland Park Midgets, the Engelettes would come out on the short end of an 11-2 score, getting but two hits off the opposing pitcher.

The final league game for the Engelettes game of the year took place on August 23 versus the Peerless team. Behind the hitting of Mitchell who singled, doubled and tripled, the Engelettes took a 9-6 win. However, it did not change the final standings of the league and the Engelettes would end their first season with a league mark of 4-10.

Although the league season had ended, the Engelettes continued to play games against male teams. On back to back days, August 26 and 27, they defeated Lakeview by a score of 12-6 and the East Lake Swans, 12-11. Game reports do not mention if Jackie played in either contest. The newspaper reported that The Engelettes would face two more Tennessee opponents, a boys' team from Dayton and an all-girls team at Lafayette on August 28 and September 1, respectively. However there were no games results published for either contest

On September 3, the Engelettes traveled to play a team from Summerville, Georgia. They dropped the contest by a score of 15-14. Again, there was no mention of Jackie playing in that game.

Jackie's last appearance of the season on the mound was against the local Buster Brown team on September 13. The Engelettes came out on top by a score of 9-8. Jackie started the game and struck out nine batters in getting the victory. She also got three hits in the game.

The season would end with the Engelettes having an overall record of 7-13, with Jackie finishing with a pitching record of 3-5.

CHAPTER 3
From the Hardwood to the Diamond

Between the 1930 and 1931 baseball season, Jackie would take to the basketball court. Her team, the Mitchellettes (sponsored by her father) got an early jump on the season, playing their first contest on January 2 versus the Interstate team. It was an auspicious beginning for their season, as they dropped that game by a score of 28-12. Jackie started at guard for the Mitchellettes, but did not score.

In the 1931 yearbook for Central High School in Chattanooga, Verna B. (Jackie) Mitchell is listed as a member of the sophomore class. Pictured is the Girls' Athletic Club. Mitchell is in the middle row, fourth from the left. (Source: Chattanooga Public Library Collection)

The next day, a *Chattanooga Daily Times* article noted that the final organizational meeting for the Girl's Industrial Basketball League would take place that evening and that all games would be played on Monday nights at the Y.M.C.A.

A total of six teams would comprise the league: Mitchellettes, Standard-Thatcher, Cagettes, Alton Park, Buster Browns and the Industrial Dramatics.

During the first month and a half, Alton Park and the Mitchellettes would battle for the leagues' top spot. Jackie started at guard for most of those games. The most points she would tally for her team during the season was four points in a 51-4 drubbing of the Industrial Dramatics. Typically, Mitchell would "play a good game at guard" according to local newspaper reports. This gives the impression she was either a good ball handler or defender or possibly a combination of both.

Less than a month into the basketball season, another sports story appeared in the February 1 *Chattanooga Daily Times*. The article stated that area resident Norman "Kid" Elberfeld was preparing to open his "annual baseball school" at Almand Park in Atlanta, Georgia. In 1930, Elberfeld held his school at that location. He would conduct his 1931 classes over a 12 day period beginning on February 23, noting that each day the school would operate for nine hours a day and "longer if the boys so desire."

Elberfeld, a former major league infielder, was a longtime resident of the Chattanooga area. He had lived there since the early 1900's and in 1913, 1915-17 served as manager of the Chattanooga Lookouts minor league team.

On the surface, this story would not seem to have any impact on Jackie's basketball season. However, that would all change just three weeks later.

In late February, the Mitchellettes traveled to Scottsboro, Alabama for a game. The Mitchellettes came out on the short end of a 26-9 score with Jackie seeing playing time off the bench for her team, according the *Chattanooga Daily Times*.

That same day the newspaper announced that "Jack" Mitchell would be the first ever female attendee at the Kid Elberfeld Baseball School when it opened.

The article goes on to say that Elberfeld had been "drilling her the past week" and "taught her to throw a curve ball in five minutes." The story also notes that "Jack" had compiled an 8-3 record in the 1930 Chattanooga Girls Baseball League and also mentions that she "plays basket ball and goes in for track and swimming."

A major portion of the article also details the involvement that Joseph Mitchell has in girls' athletics. "Mitchell serves as manager for the Mitchellettes basketball team and took an active part in the September 1930 A.A.U. Southeastern women's track meet. He is even under consideration of a position on an Southeastern A.A.U. committee on women's athletics."

Elberfeld according to the article, was recently placed in charge of the American Legion baseball program in Atlanta and was under consideration by Lookouts owner Joe Engel to place him "in charge of young horsehide tossers here."

The development of this story over a several day period created more questions than answers. There is a question as to how Jackie came to the attention of Elberfeld. There is the possibility he could have seen her pitch in 1930. According to the box scores, Jackie started seven games. Jackie compiled a record of 2-4 in the girls' league and 3-5 overall, not 8-3 as was reported in the newspaper. Based on box score accounts, Jackie started seven games and completed five and struck out at least 29 batters.

Elizabeth Brandon, another left handed pitcher in the Girls League had compiled stronger numbers with a 6-4 record in the girls' league, tossing 10 complete games in 10 starts. She also hurled 74 innings and struck out 47 batters.

Additionally, one week before the announcement about Jackie going to the Baseball School, Elberfeld was already working with her. That inferred that he had decided that she would be attending his school. However, there is no context as to how the two of them connected to work on her pitching.

The other factor that comes into play is the role of Jackie's father. Some news articles mention that he had played minor league baseball. There does not seem to be any evidence to support that idea. However, his involvement as a supporter of girls' athletics in Chattanooga may have also factored into the decision of having Jackie both work with Elberfeld and be a participant at the baseball school.

During the time Jackie was attending the camp, there were no updates about how she was faring. By March 9, Jackie was back in Chattanooga preparing for a Mitchellettes game versus the Cagettes. In that game, Jackie came off the bench to play guard, but did not score. For the Mitchellettes, the Industrial League season was winding down. They would eventually finish the season with an 8-2 league mark, two games behind the Alton Park who ran the table, finishing with a record of 10-0. Following the end of regular season, a first and second team of all stars were selected by the *Chattanooga Times* League Officials. Every Alton Park team player was either a first or second team all-star selection.

The Alton Park team also played well outside of Chattanooga and by March 11, they were undefeated with a record of 26-0. The team was invited to play in an A.A.U. National Women's Basketball tournament in Dallas, Texas later in the month. The tournament would feature 34 teams from across the United States, including a Dallas, Texas club with the well-known female athlete, Mildred "Babe" Didrikson.

Locally, the City of Chattanooga rallied around the team for a number of fundraisers. One of these was a triple header basketball evening, with the feature game having Alton Park play an all-star team drawn from the other five teams in their league. That contest would be their lone loss as they ended the season 29-1, outscoring their opponents 1,077 to 317. Their 29-1 mark was the overall best of any team coming to the tourney.

The Alton Park team for the Nationals would carry the moniker, Chattanooga. On March 21, the team left for Dallas and announced their roster. All of Alton Park's eight regular season players were included as was Elizabeth Coleman, an Industrial League second team all-star from the Mitchellettes. The tenth roster spot for Dallas was taken by Jackie Mitchell. She was the lone player not selected as a first or second team league all star.

After Jackie and her team left for Dallas on March 21, a follow-up story to her time at Elberfeld's Baseball School appeared in the *Chattanooga Daily Times* the next day.

The Match 22 story "Youthful Southpaw Pitcher With Major League Hopes Stirs Interest In Girls' Baseball Throughout South," is the first mention of the Mitchell family connection to both Memphis and pitcher Dazzy Vance.

"Jack's baseball interest goes back to the time when she was barely big enough to totter around and take note of things. At that time her parents, Dr. and Mrs. Joe S. Mitchell, were living in Memphis, and it so happened that Dazzy Vance was occupying the apartment next to them. The Dazzler, at that time wearing the Chickasaw livery, was attracted to the little left-handed girl and taught her how to hold and throw a baseball."

This same article also mentions that she was the outstanding tosser in the girls' league last year and while at Kid Elberfeld's camp Jack was given "the same coaching and instructions that he did the others." The story also noted pointed out her participation in basketball as a guard on the Mitchellettes, saying "her defensive work is outstanding, but she never flashed on goal shooting."

On March 24, Chattanooga played their opening A.A.U. tournament game against a team from Casa, Arkansas. Playing their first game under girls' basketball rules (during the season the Chattanooga players played under boys' rules), they were soundly thumped by a score of 56-22. While all 10 of the Chattanooga players are listed in a box score, Mitchell is the lone player without a listed position. It's unclear how much playing time (if any) Jackie had.

The next day, Chattanooga took on the Kansas City Cubs, only to drop a 26-9 decision, ending their tournament run with a record of 0-2.

As the team headed back to Chattanooga on March 26, the newspapers across the United States announced that Jackie Mitchell would be signing a professional baseball contact with the hometown Lookouts of the Southern Association.

CHAPTER 4
Eight Days, Eleven Pitches

The Thursday March 26, 1931 *Chattanooga Daily Times* sports headline announced to the baseball world, "Jackie Mitchell, Chattanooga Girl Gets Lookout Contract – To Pitch Against Ruth."

Details of the contract had been worked out the day before by Jackie's dad, Joseph, and Lookouts owner, Joe Engel. The game plan was to have Jackie pitch one or two innings against the New York Yankees in an April 1 exhibition game. Upon returning from the A.A.U. National Tournament in Dallas, Jackie began workouts under the tutelage of coach Zinn Beck (a former major league player) and Lookouts manager, Bert Niehoff. It should be noted that Niehoff would later serve as a manager in the All American Girls Professional Baseball League.

The article mentions that Jackie's greatest ambition is to "strikeout the big Bambino and that she will be putting everything she has on the ball when she faces Ruth." The story does say that Jackie "isn't of Southern Association caliber," but is "better than many of the other young twirlers who have tried out with the Lookouts."

The story continues to tout her near perfect control, her speed and a quick breaking curve. The story also reiterated the Dazzy Vance connection, noting that he "taught Jack how to hold the ball to make it spin."

Across the United States newspapers picked up Jackie's story, and the storyline would continue to build until the day of the game. This was evidenced by the local sports page the next day with its headline: "Signing Of Girl Pitcher With The Lookouts Attracts Interest Through The Country." Most of these stories would tout the fact that Jackie was the first female to sign a professional baseball contract. However, lost along the way was that

Jackie in 1931 before the Yankee game.
(Source: Diamond Dreams Collection)

fact that Elizabeth Stride (who would play under the name of Lizzie Arlington) was the first female to sign a professional baseball contract in 1898 – 34 years earlier. Her contract was to play in the Atlantic League. On July 5, 1898, Arlington would pitch a scoreless inning in relief during a regulation league game.

As interest about Mitchell's signing continued to grow, a March 27 reporter from the Associated Press contacted Major League Baseball Commissioner Kenesaw Mountain Landis to get his take on the signing of a female player. The story noted that Landis "refused to take the matter seriously, but upon learning that Joe Engel had prepared a regulation contract for Jack Mitchell and that it would be signed on her return here from Texas, that it was all okay."

The mention of Landis' reaction itself is interesting. One of the components of the Jackie Mitchell story was that Landis voided her contract on the basis that baseball was too strenuous for females. Yet, in 1928, this same Landis supported the efforts of female infielder Margaret Gisolo's right to play baseball in an American Legion tournament.

Although the article does say that Landis had not made an official ruling on the matter, there is no evidence that he voided Jackie's contract. In fact, after Jackie's pitching appearance with the Lookouts, another female player by the name of Vada Corbus was signed by the minor league Joplin Miners in late April of 1931.

In 1934, Mildred "Babe" Didrikson appeared in three different major league spring training games, pitching a scoreless inning for the Philadelphia Athletics against the Brooklyn Dodgers on March 20. Two days later she hurled an inning for the St. Louis Cardinals against the Boston Red Sox, and finally on March 25, she tossed two scoreless innings for the Cleveland Indians against the New Orleans Pelicans.

Judge Kenesaw Mountain Landis served as the first Commissioner of Major League Baseball. According to longtime Jackie Mitchell lore, Landis voided her professional baseball contract on the basis that baseball was too strenuous for females. However, there is no documented evidence of this ban. (Source: Diamond Dreams Collection)

On June 21, 1952, Eleanor Engle was signed by the minor league Harrisburg Senators. Just a short time thereafter, National Association President George Trautman, with the support of Baseball Commissioner Ford C. Frick, canceled her contract and said that any further attempts by a team to sign a female player would face penalties.

The first ban of female players in baseball was enacted by the American Legion following the controversy surrounding Margaret Gisolo in 1928. Gisolo was the starting second baseman for her Blanford, Indiana, American Legion baseball team. When her team reached the state championship series in Indianapolis that year, an opposing team refused to take the field against Blanford because they had a female player. Landis was brought in to give his opinion on the matter (even though he had no real

Just a short time after Jackie Mitchell signed her contract with the Chattanooga Lookouts, another female baseball player, Vada Corbus, pictured at left, signed with the Joplin Miners of the Western Association on April 16, 1931. Much like the Mitchell signing, there was no indication of a ban of female ballplayers. (Source: Diamond Dreams Collection)

jurisdiction in the case). Landis came out to claim that baseball was a game for everyone and Margaret should be allowed to play (which she did).

However in June of 1929, the Legion's National Americanism Commission, officially banned females from playing in their baseball program. Gisolo, who was voted the most valuable player in the 1928 Indiana American Legion State Tournament, was invited to help present trophies for the 1929 tournament.

If Landis had voided Jackie's contract, then why would that 1931 ruling not be cited in this 1952 case, thus freeing Trautman and Frick from having to make a decision? The gentleman's agreement of not signing female baseball players lasted until 1993, when then Chicago White Sox General Manager Ron Schueler, drafted (but did not sign) his daughter Carey.

The drafting of Schueler was seen to mark an end to any bans (written or implied) on signing females to a professional baseball contract.

Prior to her appearance against the Yankees, stories surrounding Jackie started almost to spin a life of their own. Across the United States, news reports would talk about her ball playing background, where she went to school, what her future plans were and of course, the connection to Dazzy Vance.

All the while, Joe Engel, a masterful promoter was more than happy to fuel the publicity for these stories. It seemed that every minor league team wanted to trade for Jackie. Engel, of course, refused to deal his hometown star, turning down one supposed offer (reportedly to the Memphis Chicks) of two players and cash.

Jackie officially signed her contract on March 28 before many friends, family and prominent community officials. The signing was carried live on local radio and hosted by Chattanooga broadcaster, Arch McDonald. After her signing, Engel said that he saw a great future for girls baseball and that it was a "matter of time before every major league team would have their own star of the fairer sex."

Engel reportedly took out a $10,000 Volunteer State Life Insurance policy on the pitching arm of his southpaw star.

Over the next couple of days, papers across the country were still reporting on the professional baseball signing of the left-handed twirler. The day before Jackie was set to face Babe Ruth and company, the newspapers reported that Jackie "is working out in her own back yard, far from the curious. An accommodating neighbor boy is serving as catcher" and adds that "she will be kept out of sight until time to face the Yankees."

On Wednesday, April 1, Joe Engel was hoping to pack his stadium with thousands of fans who wanted to see Jackie pitch. However, Mother Nature had other plans as rain and cold caused the game to be postponed until the next day. Before the games was called however, Lookouts backstop Eddie Kenna briefly caught Jackie during a workout. According to the *Chattanooga Daily Times*, Kenna "was amazed at the ability of the little southpaw."

He also added, "She is twice as good as I imagined. Of course, she isn't ready for the Southern Association, but her signing with the Lookouts isn't a joke as some people think. Many pitchers have had a tryout with the

*In 1928, a 14-year old infielder named Margaret Gislo was one of the top players on her Blanford, Indiana American Legion baseball team. When her team reached play in the state championships, an opposing team refused to play Blanford. Baseball Commissioner Kenesaw Mountain Landis gave his support for her to continue to play. The very next year, the American Legion banned female baseball players from their program.
(Source: Diamond Dreams Collection)*

Lookouts who couldn't hurl as well as Jackie. Her control is remarkable and if she is coached along properly has a chance to make good in professional baseball."

The very next day, cooler weather was still around and the rains had subsided. The Universal Film company came out to take a series of pictures and planned to film her appearance pitching against Babe Ruth. A brief story in the April 2 *Chattanooga Daily Times* mentioned that four New York newspapermen had interviewed her and watched Jackie throw to Kenna commenting, "The Yanks had had worse pitchers trying out with them."

On April 2, 1931, 18 year old Jackie Mitchell faced one of the most feared base-ball line-ups in an exhibition game pitting the Chattanooga Lookouts and New York Yankees. From left to right are Lou Gehrig, Jackie Mitchell shaking hand with Babe Ruth as Lookouts owner Joe Engel looks on. (Source: Diamond Dreams Collection)

According to the *LaCross Tribune* (Wisconsin), "Mitchell's hearts desire is to fan the Babe and make enough money to buy a roadster."

With a large crowd on hand, the Yankees and Lookouts began the 2:30 pm tilt. With Jackie warming up along the right field stands, Lookouts starting pitcher, Clyde Barfoot, began the game surrendering a double to Yankee lead-off hitter, Earle Combs. Second place hitter, Lyn Lary, cracked a single to knock in Combs for the first Yankee run.

With a slow walk to the mound, Lookouts manager Bert Niehoff made his next move as Babe Ruth started to approach the batters box.

Once at the mound, Niehoff turned and made a motion toward where Mitchell had been throwing. Seeing the call by her manager, Jackie Mitchell crossed onto the field to the top of the mound, much to the delight of the 4,000 fans in attendance that day.

According to the newspaper reports, before stepping into the batters box, Ruth allowed Mitchell the opportunity to powder her nose.

After a deep breath, Mitchell went into her delivery. Her first pitch to Ruth was called a ball. Her next two pitches found their mark as the Bambino swung and missed them both. Afterwards, Ruth asked the umpire to take a look at the ball, apparently baffled at the low arm slot and off-speed delivery of the lefthanded Mitchell. When the umpire deemed the ball okay to continue with, Mitchell took the ball and delivered her next pitch. Ruth, maybe looking for an off-speed pitch, took a called third strike. As he was rung up, Ruth angrily tossed his bat to the side in his reaction to the strikeout.

Mitchell was not yet out of the woods as Yankee slugger Lou Gehrig was next up. With a new confidence following the strikeout of Ruth, Mitchell threw three straight pitches – all for strikes taken by Gehrig to mark the second out of the inning. Infielder Tony Lazzeri was next up. Mitchell was now on the cusp of striking out the heart of the Yankee batting order. However, after fanning Ruth and Gehrig, Jackie hit a wild streak and tossed her next four straight pitches out of the strike zone, walking Lazzeri. That was enough for manager Niehoff, who trotted out to the mound to take the ball from Mitchell and bring back in the starter Barfoot who would retire the side to ensure that no runs would be scored on Jackie.

The Yankees would however, pound out 14 hits and tally 14 runs to cop a 14-4 win over the Lookouts.

Over the next few days, newspapers across the United States published stories about Mitchell's strikeout of Ruth and Gehrig. Perhaps, one of the more interesting comments about Jackie and her accomplishment was delivered by Margaret Nabel, manager of the New York Bloomer Girls Baseball Club. The Bloomers had been playing since 1910. In 1914, Nabel joined the team as a player and in 1920, took over as manager of the club when she was 25 years old.

In an April 4, 1931, interview in the *Staten Island Advance*, Nabel offered this observation on Jackie's pitching skills. "A girl can develop a slow curve, an effective floater, good control and perhaps everything else that

JACKIE'S LOOKOUTS DALTON FOE TODAY

Big Crowd Looms for Twin Bill—Crowns, Silks Vie.

Lookout Juniors Play at Bon Air Tomorrow—Jackie to Hurl in Both Games.

Following her appearance against the Yankees, Lookouts owner Joe Engel deemed her not yet ready for play in the Southern Association. A team called the Junior Lookouts was created as a type of feeder for the minor league club. Jackie was the featured player on the team and every so often, newspapers referred to the team as "Jackie's Lookouts". (Source: Chattanooga Daily Times, *May 16, 1931)*

a good male player can show, except speed," Nabel said. "While I wish my Tennessee colleague every success, it seems it is just another publicity stunt," she went on to add.

Nabel's club early on, as many Bloomer teams often did, featured a male pitcher and catcher. Over time, she would however use a female pitcher against other female Bloomer teams.

Although Nabel did not witness Jackie pitching against Ruth and Gehrig, she must have felt that she needed to see Jackie pitch firsthand.

At the end of May, the New York Bloomer Girls would make a trip to Chattanooga to see Jackie play.

CHAPTER 5
The Junior Lookouts

For the next two weeks following Mitchell's appearance against the Yankees, newspapers across the United States still were mentioning her performance. Still, there did not seem to be a plan as to what Jackie would be doing next. While under contract with the Lookouts, it was unsure if she might only be available for home games or if she would be around for the entire 1931 Lookouts season.

Around April 18, part of Jackie's future had already been decided. According to numerous newspaper accounts, Jackie would for sure not travel with the Lookouts in 1931. In these accounts according to Lookouts owner Joe Engel, Jackie, "was not up to the task of taking a regular turn on the mound." Engel went on to add, "Next year, maybe." Those comments appeared to evaporate the professional baseball aspirations of Mitchell. However, the next part of her baseball journey was about to begin.

On April 30, the *Chattanooga Daily Times* announced that Kid Elberfeld, Jackie's baseball school instructor, was named by Engel as manager of a team called the Junior Lookouts. Before this formal announcement, Elberfeld had been already running workouts for the team which would include Jackie. Engel along with Jackie's dad, Joe Mitchell, would plan a schedule for some 75 games across the south.

According to the story, the team would have, "many of the best rookies who turned out for the Lookout school this spring and couldn't be placed on account of the breaking up of so many smaller leagues, will get more experience with the Juniors. The best of them will get new trials with the Lookouts next spring."

NEW YORK BLOOMER GIRLS, Margaret R. Nabel, Mgr.
77 VAN DUZER STREET, STATEN ISLAND, N. Y.

5. Julie Gressek; 6. Dotty Ruh; 1. Helen Demarest; 2. Hattie Michaels; 10. Ginger Robinson
4. Alma Pucci; 7. Margaret Nabel; 9. Edna Lockhart; 8. Mary Ontek; 3. Mel Pearsall.

Jackie's appearance against the Yankees drew commentary from all across the world of baseball. Margaret Nabel, manager of the New York Bloomer Girls wished her success and in a rare trek to Tennessee, brought her team to play against Jackie and the Lookouts. This Bloomer image is a photo postcard used to publicize their ballclub.(Source: Diamond Dreams Collection)

Throughout the early part of the 1931 season, the names "Junior Lookouts" and "Jackie Mitchell's Junior Lookouts" were used interchangeably in newspaper reports. The club opened its season on May 6 at Alcoa, Tennessee. Before 400 fans, Jackie would get the start, toss one inning, give up two runs, but was not the pitcher of record in a 10-9 loss. Two days later, The Junior Lookouts were playing at Lenoir City. The team won that day by a score of 4-3. Jackie did not make an appearance on the mound, but played in right field, getting one hit in two trips to the plate.

On Saturday May 9, Jackie was back on the hill against the Penn-Dixies of Richard City. Although the team would end up with a 12-5 win, Jackie would not get a decision for her three innings of work. She surrendered one hit and issued one walk. Before the start of the game, Jackie was presented a bouquet of flowers.

The next day, Mitchell was again the starter on the mound, hurling but one inning and giving up two hits in another no decision, although her team would finish on top by a 14-8 score. At bat, Mitchell was walked once, but left the game with a sore arm. The next day, the Junior Lookouts played the Chattanooga City League Peerless team at Engel Stadium. They would win by a 5-4 score, but Mitchell did not play.

Mitchell would bounce back on May 14 for another start. She surrendered but one hit, although it's not clear how many innings Jackie pitched that day. The Junior Lookouts won that day by a 34-6 margin.

Against a team from Dalton, Georgia on May 16, Jackie took her turn on the mound, tossing one inning, giving up four hits and three runs in getting her first loss of the season as her team lost 18-6.

The very next day, Jackie again got the start at Bon Air, Tennessee. She hurled two innings, giving up one hit and three runs. Again, she was saddled with a no decision, despite her team winning by a score of 14-10.

A week went by before the Junior Lookouts were again in action. Mitchell for her part had started season the mound in six of the teams' first eight games, but only twice tossing more than one inning.

Mitchell got the starting nod on May 24 when the Junior Lookouts traveled to Tullahoma, Tennessee. In that outing, she was touched up for three hits and three runs and took her second loss of the season. Four days later in Sewanee, Tennessee, Jackie started on the mound for the eighth time in ten games. She surrendered two hits and a run, but again did not get a decision in a 13-3 Junior Lookout victory.

The day Jackie and her team headed to Sewanee, the *Chattanooga Times* announced a first-ever appearance in Chattanooga by the New York Bloomer Girls. They would take on Jackie and her club at Engel Stadium on May 30. The Bloomers were managed by Margaret Nabel and had traversed the United States since 1910. They featured some of the most talent female baseball players including such as third baseman Ginger Robinson and second sacker Ethel Condon. On that same date, a local baseball note detailed an appearance by lefthanded pitcher Elizabeth Brandon, who was a rival hurler of Jackie's in the Chattanooga Girls Baseball League in 1930 as a member of the Peerless team. Brandon was just been signed by the St. Elmo team in Chattanooga and became the first girl to break into the local amateur league when she gave up only five hits and struck out six batters in seven innings of work against Boynton.

The game against the Bloomers would mark Jackie's first appearance on the mound in Engel Stadium since striking out Babe Ruth and Lou Gehrig on April 2. It would also mark the first time she would be facing an all-female baseball team since an August 9, 1930, 17-4 loss to Soddy Hosiery of the Chattanooga Girls Baseball League.

Against the Bloomers, Jackie was up to the task. In her best outing of 1931, she held the veteran barnstorming team hitless in the first three innings of the game. The Junior Lookouts aided her start, scoring seven times to top the Bloomers by a score of 7-4. Although, pitching her best game of the season, Jackie, again did not get a decision in the nine inning contest. According to the local newspaper, "Jackie retired at the beginning of the fourth, as she is to show her wares daily for the next two weeks in other towns and it is necessary that she work only a few innings a day."

There are a number of instances following an outstanding performance by an opposing female baseball player, Nabel would try to sign that player for her team. Despite Jackie's work against the New York Bloomers, there does not seem to be any indication that they attempted to lure her from the Junior Lookout roster.

That same day, the newspaper reported that the Junior Lookouts would begin a trip that would see them play 10 games in six different states, beginning with a May 3 doubleheader in Dyersburg, Tennessee.

Another story detailed the fact that Tullahoma Independents had just signed Christy Sears. According to the newspaper, Sears had been away at the Teacher's College in Murfreesboro, Tennessee and just missed meeting Jackie in her recent game at Tullahoma. Sears, an outstanding basketball player as well, had recently broke the college girls' baseball throwing record with a toss of 223 feet, six inches. The story went on to add that, "she has played baseball with kids and school teams all her life."

The Junior Lookouts opened their long road trip in Dyersburg with a 6-5 win in 10 innings. Jackie started on the hill and tossed a scoreless first inning. The second game did not go as well as the Junior Lookouts lost by a 15-1 margin. Mitchell did not play in that second game.

In the June 3 game versus Athens, Alabama, Jackie again was the starting pitcher, surrendering a pair of hits in her inning of work as the Junior Lookouts won by a score of 10-4. For the second straight day, Jackie was the opening hurler for the Junior Lookouts as her club lost to the Florence, Alabama nine on June 4, by a score of 7-4. Jackie threw the first two innings, striking out a pair of batters.

For the third straight game, Jackie took to the hill to face the Lincoln Mills team from Huntsville, Alabama. As in her previous appearances, she would get the start. In this game, Jackie threw the first inning, allowing one run as the Junior Lookouts won by a score of 5-4. She made it four straight starts on June 6 in Sheffield, Alabama, against the Southern Railway nine. Jackie worked a scoreless first inning based on newspaper accounts. Immediately following that game, Jackie and her club headed to Memphis, Tennessee for a doubleheader.

The Junior Lookouts arrived in Memphis with a record of 11-6. The *Memphis Commercial Appeal* ran a June 7 game day look at the twin bill between the Junior Lookouts and Memphis Steam Laundry in game one and the second contest that pitted the visitors against undefeated Jolly Cabs. A local Memphis player named Lee Wilkinson would be the catcher for the Junior Lookouts that day. And the Steam Laundry team announced the addition of High School Catholic baseball star, Thomas "Red" Savori to its roster.

None of the local newspapers mentioned that Jackie Mitchell and her family had resided in Memphis. There was also no mention of former Memphis Chicks pitcher Dazzy Vance teaching Jackie to pitch.

The wear and tear of five straight days of being the starting pitcher was beginning to take a toll on Mitchell as she took the mound in the first inning against Steam Laundry. She would last but two innings, surrendering five hits and five runs. The Junior Lookouts would eventually win the game by a 12-10 score. Jackie would come back to start the second game was well but would last only one inning, surrendering two runs on two hits in getting the loss in an 11-2 decision versus the Jolly Cabs. Mitchell would have only one strikeout on the day, that being in the first game versus "Red' Savori.

Following a couple of days off, the Junior Lookouts traveled to Columbus, Mississippi to battle the Columbus Creamery nine. It would also marked the seventh straight game that Mitchell would start. In a 7-6 win for the Junior Lookouts, Jackie would throw a scoreless first inning.

Continuing their swing through the south, the Junior Lookouts took on the Louisville and Nashville Railroad team on June 12 in Gadsden, Alabama. Mitchell continued her string of consecutive game starts, hurling two scoreless innings, surrendering just a single hit, while her team won its 14th game by a score of 11-2.

With Junior Lookouts' long road trip over, Mitchell started to field offers from teams outside of Chattanooga. The first such offer was from a semi-pro team in Lexington, Kentucky.

Newspaper accounts noted that Jackie started the July 14 game for the hometown team and did not allow a ball to be hit out of the infield in the first two innings. She would give up a hit, a base on balls and allow a run in the third inning before leaving the game.

Following her appearance in Lexington, Jackie returned to her mound duties with the Junior Lookouts. Over the next week, she would start four games. In at least two of those games she would hurl two innings. In her first two-inning stint on June 19, she allowed six runs. In Jackie's June 21 two-inning appearance, she did not surrender a hit. All four games were won by the Junior Lookouts. However, all four were no decisions for Jackie.

On Friday, June 26, Jackie was booked (as a solo again), to pitch for a local picked nine in Atlanta, Georgia..

For Jackie, it would be the first night game that she would ever pitch in. Before the game took place however, her family's car was broken into resulting in the loss of all of her clothes, including her uniform and brand new baseball glove.

Once she replaced her uniform and glove, Jackie started the game, pitching the first three innings, surrendering four runs, but not figuring in the decision in her teams' 7-5 win. The newspaper said that Jackie would be back in town with the Junior Lookouts for a July 4 game.

Following her return from Atlanta, Jackie and the Junior Lookouts were slated to travel to Tullahoma, Tennessee on Sunday, June 28. This game was to feature a battle of female twirlers as Jackie would face Tullahoma pitcher Christy Sears.

Tullahoma had defeated the Junior Lookouts by a score of 8-5 in their only previous meeting. The game report for the most recent match-up mentioned that the game "was a disappointment to the big crowd of sweltering fans." There was no mention of either Jackie or Christy Sears playing that day.

The July 3 *Chattanooga Times* reported that the Junior Lookouts had added a pair of outfielders for their upcoming game against Dalton, Georgia and a July 4 contest versus Bon Air. There were no results listed for the Dalton game and although Jackie reportedly traveled with the Junior Lookouts for those games, she is not mentioned as to having played. The Junior Lookouts and Bon Air played to an 0-0 tie before the game was called due to rain.

The Lookout Juniors continued with their road games, looking to take on Crossville, Georgia with Jackie again on the mound. However, there is no mention of Jackie making the trip to Crossville. The Junior Lookouts won the game by a 6-3 score.

Right after that game result, the newspaper announced that Junior Lookouts have played their least game under the name "Junior Lookouts" and that they would continue to play the season "without Jackie Mitchell in the lineup." The team would now be known as the Chattanooga Stars and would still be led by Kid Elberfeld.

On July 14, the *Chattanooga Times* explained that the change to the team were made because of the "constant demand for Jackie's services by other teams." The former Lookouts would play under the moniker of Elberfeld's All-Stars.

CHAPTER 6
Jackie Goes Solo

After parting with the Junior Lookouts, Jackie Mitchell would embark on a baseball journey as a player without a traditional team. Although she had from time to time pitched for a non-Chattanooga team, Jackie would now travel the baseball road solo, assisting any team wanting to hire her to pitch a couple of innings for their club.

That first step for her, according to the newspaper, would be pitching for the Knoxville (Tennessee) Reds on July 14, before going to Morristown, Tennessee, and Cleveland, Ohio. She would then embark on a Midwest circuit which would include: Manhattan and Wichita, Kansas; Helena, Arkansas, Council Bluffs and Davenport, Iowa along with 15 additional cities.

On July 12, 1931, the *Knoxville News Sentinel*, mentioned that after her appearance against the Yankees, had been put on the "non-playing list" by the Lookouts and had been recently signed by "Doc" Jenkins, manager of the Federal Clothiers team to pitch for his club. No box score or results have been found for this game.

After Knoxville, Morristown, Tennessee would be her next stop. The *Morristown Gazette* announced that Jackie would be starting on the mound for the local Junior Order team against the Knoxville Fireman on July 15. Local shop owners were closing all of their businesses on that afternoon as the game, "promises to be one of the best ever played in Morristown."

One of the largest crowds of the season saw Jackie start the game for the Junior Order team and set down the first three hitters for Knoxville in the first inning. In the second inning however, The Firemen managed a pair of hits off Jackie and couple with two defensive miscues from her club, the

Firemen scored all three of their runs in that frame. Morristown however would score eight runs on the day to defeat the Firemen by a score of 8-3.

Following the game, manager Paxton of the Junior Order announced that Jackie had signed up to play four games with the Juniors, beginning on July 29. The planned slate would include games in Greenville, Newport, Johnson City and Middlesboro, Tennessee.

After leaving Morristown, Jackie arrived in Cleveland on July 17. The next day, the *Cleveland Plain Dealer*, announced that Jackie would pitch in a three-game series. On the first night against Jack Graney's Nighthawks, she would "don an Akron Goodyear uniform," and that "the uniform incidentally will not entirely conceal the fact that Jackie is a very feminine young woman with charm and an abundance of good looks." Opposing Jackie on the mound would be another female hurler from the Cleveland area who would be selected by Graney. When asked about her strikeouts of Babe Ruth and Lou Gehrig back in April, Mitchell replied, "There was an element of satisfaction, but no thrill."

The newspaper also noted that Mitchell "had been granted a leave by the Chattanooga Southern League Club, with which she is signed as a regular pitcher, so she can tour the north and Midwest."

Pitching in only the second night game of her career the next day, Mitchell hurled two scoreless innings with one strikeout. Her mound opponent, Margaret Kelly, also hurled two scoreless innings and struck out Mitchell in her only at bat. Although she did not get a decision, the Nighthawks won the game by a score of 4-3.

Much of the newspaper account of the game compared the differences between Mitchell and Kelly. The story noted that "Pitcher Mitchell had a more boyish figure than pitcher Kelly" and that "pitcher Kelly's hair was much prettier than pitcher Mitchell's."

The entrance for the two female pitchers to the ballpark were made quite differently as well. Mitchell "came to the park all set to go to work" while, "pitcher Kelly arrived in French heels and a long brown frock."

The very next day, Mitchell was back on the mound, this time wearing the uniform of the Graney Nighthawks. She opposed the Goodyear team, who at least on that day, also had a female pitcher by the name of Hockman.

Mitchell tossed two scoreless innings and struck out one batter, matching her performance of the game before. The Nighthawks, despite her two solid innings, lost the game by a score of 10-0.

The very last game for Jackie in Cleveland took place on July 22. For that game, she would hurl for the Kilbane Playboys against the Graney Nighthawks. The newspaper stated that in her four innings of work while in Cleveland, Jackie had not surrendered a run, struck out two batters and had only given up one hit. However, there was no box or linescore for the Playboys-Nighthawks game.

Following the series in Cleveland, Mitchell would next head to Middlesboro, Kentucky for a July 29 game. Jackie would be on the mound for Middlesboro as they took on Pineville. This was a benefit game for the Middlesboro Kiwanis Club, with all the proceeds to go to the local Boy Scouts. It was noted in the *Middlesboro Daily News*, that "special permission from her owners had to be obtained for her to play here."

The day before she was slated to pitch in Middlesboro, Jackie paid a visit to Clarence Kirby, the World's Champion Tree Sitter. The story of the two celebrities was page one news in Middlesboro. Kirby had been living for the past month and a half in his tree home to claim a world's record for tree sitting. The newspaper reported that Jackie, "climbed up into the tree and inspected the home and also gave Clarence an autographed base ball." The event was captured by photographer Allen C. Cooke of the Tri-State Studio, who snapped a shot of both Jackie and Clarence on the front porch of the tree house.

Much like the playing date in Morristown, "Most of the merchants closed their stores and called it a half-day holiday," according the Morristown newspaper. "Approximately 800 fans witnessed the game" which was the largest crowd to see a baseball game in years.

Jackie pitched the first and ninth inning for the Middlesboro Boosters as they took on their opponents from Pineville. In the first frame, Pineville scored four times. In the next seven innings, the Boosters would rally to take a 7-5 lead. However, Pineville was again able to get to Mitchell in her second inning of work by scoring two runs to tie the score 7-7 at the end of nine innings. In the 10th inning, the Boosters would hold Pineville scoreless and tally a run in the bottom of the inning for an 8-7 win.

Following the game in Middlesboro, Jackie returned to the Morristown Junior Order club for their game against the Johnson City (Tennessee) Juniors. Jackie started the game in Johnson City and pitched two innings, surrendering two runs and giving up a base on balls. Although behind when she left the game, Morristown would rally for an 8-3 win.

As the baseball season was winding down for Jackie, the August 6 *Plain Speaker* newspaper in Hazleton, Pennsylvania, stated that soon she and "her all star team of former major leaguers" would be playing a series of games against Eastern League teams.

Over the next few days, updates would be reported in the newspaper. On August 13, it was mentioned that a game against Allentown, "has been postponed due to the girl pitcher and her team being unable to appear until August 26."

Other than the stories in the Hazleton newspaper regarding Jackie's team, there does not seem to be an indication that such a club even existed as there are no additional stories talking about other games or the make-up as to who the "former major leaguers" were.

Following the end of the baseball season, Jackie would get ready to play basketball. In the December 8, *Chattanooga Daily Times*, a story announces the formation of a new basketball team called the Lookout Mountaineers. The team was sponsored by Joseph Mitchell, Jackie's father. She would be the only female player on the team and would serve as its captain. The team was formerly known as the Mitchell's and had won the Chattanooga city independent championship the previous season.

According to the story, the team would be comprised of, "Ted Rogers, Earl Hazel, Ish Moore, Bob Owen, James Sivley and Harry King" and went on to add that, "Jackie Mitchell, Chattanooga's feminine contribution to baseball, is to direct the newly formed outfit and will play in all its games. Jackie was a member of Chattanooga's entry in the National A.A.U. women's tourney at Dallas, Tex., last year. Her play in this tournament received extensive mention. Only Chattanooga's early elimination kept her from making the mythical All-American."

The Mountaineers opened their season on December 15 at Trion, Georgia, but fell by a score of 27-18. The *Chattanooga Daily Times* game report noted that, "Jackie Mitchell entered the game late in the second half, but was unable to render much aid to the losing cause." For the second straight day, the Mountaineers were on the road, this time in Dunlap, Tennessee, where they would beat the home team, 42-32. Jackie would play the fourth quarter, but did not score. The next game for the Mountaineers was a December 17 contest in Jackson, Tennessee against the Smith Health Club. The Mountaineers would drop that game by a 29-14 margin. Jackie played the third period for her team. Two days later, the Mountaineers traveled to play against the Earle (Arkansas) Cardinals. They would notch their second win of the season by a score of 29-8. During the rest of December, Mitchell would play periodically in games for the team. Near the end of the month the local newspaper mentioned that the team has recently returned from a 10 game, 11-day trip and had complied a record of 5-5 during that time.

On March 19, the *Chattanooga Daily Times* reported that the Mountaineers would be playing at Summerville, Georgia that evening. "Boone, Marmon, Moore, Hazel, T. Rogers and Jackie Mitchell would be making that trip." The Mountaineers would win the game by a score of 29-26, but there was no mention of Mitchell playing in the game.

CHAPTER 7
The Piedmont League

As the 1932 baseball season began, Jackie Mitchell, was in the process of finishing up her junior year at Central High School in Chattanooga. As the school year was coming to an end, Chattanooga, like other communities were getting ready for summer activities at their parks.

Financially, the Great Depression was still at hand. Chattanooga was struggling with a way to pay its park supervisors for the upcoming summer. A May 24 article in the *Chattanooga Daily Times*, stated that Parks Commissioner James A. Cash would reject the idea of using volunteer supervisors for the city playgrounds. According to the story, Cash's statement, "followed the receipt of a letter from Miss Jackie Mitchell, Central High School student and professional baseball player, offering to organize a volunteer corps of high school girls to work on the playgrounds." The story went on to say that Cash was worried about how a volunteer could control the children and park equipment when he rejected the Mitchell proposal. When the Chattanooga playgrounds did reopen, Jackie was listed as a substitute director.

On July 23, the *Chattanooga Daily Times* featured two different mentions of Jackie. While at the Elizabeth Lupton Y.W.C.A. summer recreation center in White Sulphur Springs, Georgia, Jackie played in a camp baseball game that drew everyone who was attending camp. "Campers and counselors went as spectators anxious to see in action the girl who 'fanned Babe Ruth' in a Chattanooga baseball game."

In that same paper was an article saying that "Jackie Mitchell Plans Eastern Baseball Tour." According to the story, Jackie would depart on

August 1 and that the tour would last for ten weeks. The most interest-ing mention in the story was that an (unnamed) "Cleveland (O.) booking agent" would be making the arrangements for the tour.

Prior to her signing with the agent, Jackie's non-Junior Lookouts' pitching performances in 1931, were arranged by her father, Joseph.

In early August of 1932, newspapers reported that Jackie Mitchell had signed a unique contract with the Piedmont League, a Class B minor league circuit. According to R.J. (Russell) Schlueter, a representative of the Chattanooga baseball club, Jackie is "booked for appearances at all of the Piedmont League parks." She will pitch for each team at home, rather than pitching for a single member of the league. According to Schlueter, "Jackie is really on the Chattanooga club roster. Three major league clubs have sought to buy her contract and one club, offered $8,000 for her for use in exhibitions and on spring training tours."

It is not clear as to exactly when Schlueter became involved with the Chattanooga club and the booking of Mitchell's appearances. He is the first named person (outside of the family) to be associated with serving to pro-mote or act as an agent for Jackie.

Schlueter was a native of Richmond, Virginia. The 44-year-old had been a promoter of sorts in and around the Richmond area. Not all of his ventures were successful. In October of 1925, Schlueter filed for bankrupt-cy in Richmond. A few years later, in 1928, he served as a promoter for Joe Whitney, Hawaiian Entertainer.

At the beginning of the 1932 season, the Piedmont League was com-prised of eight teams. As with a number of minor leagues that year, there were financial difficulties. By the time Jackie signed her contract with the league, the league was down to six teams and struggling to survive.

One such example of those struggles involved the Raleigh Capitals. In late August, the Capitals were slated to play the Greensboro Patriots. How-ever, before the game, there were only 50 paid fans. There was not enough money to cover the $25 field rental along with additional costs for the lights to play, so the game was rescheduled as a doubleheader the next day.

Unlike Jackie's previous appearances, her mound time in the Pied-mont League would be exhibition only. She would "start" for the home team and hurl two to three innings either before or between games of a double-header.

Her first league appearance was for the Durham Bulls against the Raleigh on August 13. According to the *High Point Enterprise*, "The clubs staged a two-inning exhibition contest prior to the regular game in which Miss Jackie Mitchell, Tennessee girl southpaw, worked on the mound for the Bulls." The next day, Mitchell threw two innings for the Raleigh Caps against the Winston-Salem Twins.

Jackie's next game would be for the league leading Charlotte Hornets on August 18, as they faced Raleigh. The *Charlotte Observer* noted that the Hornets topped the Capitals by a score of 6-0 in seven innings, "to make room for a three-inning exhibition, featuring Jackie Mitchell, 18 year old girl pitcher and the property of the Chattanooga Southern League club."

The newspaper described Jackie's appearance this way: "Jackie twirled for the home club and "won" her game by the score of 4-2. There was much clowning as the Capitals considerately allowed hits to trickle through them at the right time. Jackie got an infield hit and scored the run that put the Hornets ahead after the visitors had paved the way for her all the way around the bases."

On August 20, Jackie took to the hill for a two-inning stint for the High Point Pointers following their seven inning, 11-6 win over Wilmington. The *High Point Enterprise*, reported that, "A burlesque two-innings in which Miss Jackie Mitchell, youthful girl pitcher for the Chattanooga Lookouts, performed on the mound, supplied semi-comic relief for the fans after the seven slow innings that had preceded. Miss Mitchell did well enough with her twirling, but owing to the levity with which the players on both teams seemed to regard the occasion, her test was not a fair one."

Jackie's final appearance for the Piedmont League was on August 23. That day, she threw two exhibition innings for the Greensboro Patriots before their regular game against Durham. The *Greensboro Record* reported that, "Miss Jackie Mitchell, girl 'wonder' hurler, performed on the mound for the Pats. The girl not only proved that she could throw a baseball, but she could get on base being issued a free pass."

A February 12, 1933 *Chattanooga Daily Times* feature article about Jackie reflected on her time in the Piedmont League this way: " Jackie's value as a box office attraction is evident in gate receipts wherever she plays, and she helped pull several clubs in the Piedmont League out of the red last season, where she played a series of games. Judge Brabham, president of the Piedmont League, recognized Jackie's drawing power and credited her with much of the financial success of the league last season."

Following her last game with Piedmont League teams, Jackie had one more outing in that area. On August 19, the *High Point Enterprise* reported that, "Jackie Mitchell girl pitcher from the Chattanooga Lookouts and a unique hurler in the fact that she is the only girl twirler under contract in America, has been signed by (Thomas Mills Tommies) Manager Yow. The Tennessee moundsman will play by special permission of the Chattanooga management."

Jackie would start and throw the first two innings for the Tommies, giving up two hits and a run, it was later decided that those two innings would not count in their 7-1 loss to Proximity.

That same day, in a number of newspapers across the United States, the was a brief Associated Press story which said, "Jackie Mitchell, Memphis girl pitcher, who broke into fame last year by fanning Babe Ruth and Lou Gehrig and who was ruled out of baseball by Judge K.M. Landis has taken to barnstorming. She has appeared in exhibition games at various cities over the south with semi-pro clubs."

This is the first time where there is a reference in print of Landis ruling her out of baseball.

After pitching a series of exhibitions, Mitchell and her manager R.J. Schlueter decided to finish her eastern swing with a number of games in Virginia.

Her first game would be on the mound for the Martin Sales team of Richmond on August 30. On August 28, a *Richmond Times* writer named David Lidman wrote an article giving some background for Jackie's upcoming appearance. Lidman starts out his story with, "Jackie Mitchell is going to be a major league pitcher. She says so—but Judge Landis says maybe not." In his last paragraph he writes," Then in the spring of 1931 Joe Engel, a real showman and the type of club owner the minor leagues need saw the crowd-drawing possibilities in the girl pitcher. He signed her up. Joe planned to make her a regular member of his Chattanooga team and carry her on trips over the circuit to help pack 'em in other towns but Judge Kenesaw Landis ruled a woman had no place in organized baseball. That was that."

Jackie threw three innings for Martin Sales in their August 30, 10-9 win over Church Hill. She would surrender two hits and one run. The headline in August 31 *Richmond Times* game account read, "Babe Mitchell Hurl In Sales' Victory." This would be the first time that Jackie would be referred to by that name. In that same issue of the newspaper, a writer by the name of Lily Mae Freeman wrote a feature story about Jackie. Freeman touched on a number of subjects, stating that, "She (Jackie) had received many offers to join various teams, including the New York Bloomer Girls, but so far she has preferred to remain independent and finish her education." Freeman also reported that, "Jackie is branching out into the field of aeronautics. Under Al Hoffman of Salisbury, North Carolina, she is learning to fly. She has already taken the plane up and brought it down alone, and soon hopes to get back to her plane and obtain a pilot's license."

FULL-VUE BASKET BALL TEAM.
Left to Right—R. J. Schlueter, manager; Jackie Mitchell, guard; Margie Carson, forward; Vern Fisher, forward; Katherine Eppert, center; Elizabeth Brown, center; Mary Lee Sparks, guard. Elizabeth Coleman, guard, and Virginia Parish, forward, are not in the picture.

During the winter of 1932-33, Jackie played basketball for two Chattanooga teams, the Lookouts and Full-Vues. The Full-Vues were organized by her then agent-business manager R. J. Schlueter. (Source: Chattanooga Daily Times, *December 11, 1932)*

Her next outing would be on the mound for the Suffolk Athletic Club for a September 4 game against Deep Creek. That day, Jackie would start, throw three innings, while giving up four hits and two runs as Suffolk would win the game by a 13-3 score. The next start for Jackie was her shortest and least effective outing of her eastern trip. While starting for the Waddey ballclub against the St. Mary's Celtics, Jackie would only last an inning and a third, allowing four walks and a pair of runs.

On September 10, Jackie would make the last start of her trip. This time she would be on the mound for the Norfolk Orioles as they took on the Naval Hospital Medics. Jackie would give up seven runs in that game while pitching the first three innings. It would be her only game of record (a loss) on her trip.

By September 13, Jackie, her parents and manager, R. J. Schlueter are back home and the *Chattanooga Daily Times* reported that, "Three movie firms in Hollywood have made Jackie offers to take a part in a baseball picture, but she has not yet decided which one to accept."

As the 1932 baseball season was drawing to a close for Jackie, a controversy arose regarding gate receipts for a game that had been slated to take place in Nashville, Tennessee on October 9. Jackie was scheduled to pitch against a Nashville All-Star team. According to the *Nashville Banner* on October 11, "Jackie's manager contended that she signed a contract calling for 50 per cent of the gate and that she was entitled to the jack whether or not she appeared in the game." However, it seemed that the Nashville team balked at Jackie receiving such a large financial cut from the game receipts.

Although the game was slated for an afternoon start, apparently promoters for the game announced that the teams were to play at 9:00 am on October 9 and when Mitchell did not show up at that time, the organizers deemed that her contract was canceled.

After the game ended without Jackie playing, Schlueter took the game receipts which came to $189.70 to a local magistrate on Jackie's behalf. On Monday, October 10, Squire Binns ruled against Jackie, saying that, "she had no contract with Moose Clabaugh who handled the game."

As the case in previous off seasons, once baseball season had concluded, Jackie was ready to turn her attention to the hardwood. The *Chattanooga Daily Times* reported that the Jackie Mitchell's Lookout Mountaineers, would start a barnstorming tour on December 1 and that they had

Jackie Mitchell.

Between baseball seasons, it was not uncommon to find Jackie on a basketball court. Before her appearance against the New York Yankees, she had been playing in an Amateur Athletic Union (AAU) national tourney in Dallas, Texas. Jackie is generally described as a good "defensive" player. (Source: Chattanooga Daily Times, November 6, 1932)

just started to practice at the Central Y.M.C.A. It would be Jackie's second winter with the team.

Along with Jackie, the team would consist of: Frank Blakely, Central High School; Lewis Tucker, University of Chattanooga; Buck Adams, Tennessee Wesleyan; Lester Newton, Carson-Newman; Earl Hazel and Ish Moore of Red Bank. R. J. Schlueter would serve as manager.

A couple of days later, it was announced that Charlotte Hornets baseball manager Guy Lacy would lead the Mountaineers while Schlueter would now serve as business manager.

Earlier in the fall, there was talk about Jackie's participation in movies. However, a *Chattanooga Daily Times* story on November 6, said that Jackie had turned down offers to enter the movies and would instead, according to her father and manager, "finish her education and pitch baseball during the summer to help finance her college course."

Although Jackie had planned to play basketball for the Lookout Mountaineers for a second season, a November 29 story in the *Chattanooga Daily Times*, announced that Jackie would head up a new, all-female basketball team which would be sponsored by the Loveman optical department. According to the story, the "Loveman's are seeking games both in and out of town. In addition to Miss Mitchell, the following girls are now members of the team: Toots Brown, Katherine Eppert, Virginia Paris, Margaret Carson and Elizabeth Coleman." This new team, managed by Schlueter, would be called the Full-Vues.

Mitchell's new team opened its basketball season on December 13 against the Erlanger Nurses and came out on the short end of a 24-6 score. In that game, Jackie tallied four points. Their second game was a 30-21 loss against the Bacon Hosiery Mills a couple of days later. Mitchell finished that game with three points.

With the start of a new year, it was hoped that the fortune of the Full-Vues would turn around. However, on January 2, the team suffered a 52-11 loss to Peerless, a strong city league team. Before their next game, the Full-Vues would suffer a different kind of loss as two of its players would leave the team to join other clubs. Margaret Mason would join the Peerless team while Virginia Paris joined the Bacon Hosiery Mill team. The next two games continued to see the Full-Vues struggle as they dropped a 41-32 game versus the Cleveland Bacons as well as a 46-37 clash against Dayton on January 14.

The Full-Vues took to the road and would travel to Cleveland, Tennessee to face the Bacon Hosiery Mills team on January 17. Jackie came off the bench to score four points in a 38-28 loss. The team would continue its tailspin, dropping back to back games on January 21 and 22, losing first to the Dunlap Independents by a score of 35-30 and then to the Kingston Blues by a score of 30-28. According to the Kingston game report, Mitchell and Carson were the high scorers. According to the "Cage Notes" column in the January 27, *Chattanooga Daily Times*, the Full-Vues "want to secure a tall center." Near the end of January, the Full-Vues would meet the Charles H. Bacon company in Lenoir City, Tennessee. That January 29 game had the Full-Vues tagged with another loss, this time by a score of 41-20. Mitchell, who started the game at center, scored a single point.

After nine consecutive losses, the Full-Vues would break into the win column in a big way. On January 30, they throttled the Y.M.H.A by a score of 42-19 and followed that up two days later against the same team, this time by a score of 85-6. The Full-Vues would win a third straight game on February 3, this time defeating First Baptist, 28-4. Their three game win streak would end however the very next day as they dropped a 21-9 game versus the Erlanger Nurses.

In their next game versus the Millers on February 7, the newspaper reported that after two Full-Vues players had fouled out, the Millers withdrew a player from the court so that the game would finish evenly. No score for this game was given. Away from the basketball court, Jackie was again in the news.

On February 12, 1933, the *Chattanooga Daily Times* featured a photograph of Raymond McDonald, who at 18 years of age, was Chattanooga's youngest pilot having just received his license. Jackie, pictured next to him and the plane was according to the paper, "his first passenger."

A little more than a week later, the Full-Vues traveled to Dalton, Georgia, where they would drop their game by a score of 50-27. Jackie played center in the game and tallied six points. The final regular season game for the Full-Vues was a February 17 game on the road against the Independents in Oneida, Tennessee. They would lose this final regular season game by a score of 36-22 loss and finish with a record of 3-12.

Near the end of the basketball season, an eight-team tournament was scheduled to be played to determine an East Tennessee champion. The tournament would be played under the National A.A.U. (Amateur Athletic Union) rules. Originally, it was thought that there would be 16 entrants, but that number was whittled down to eight.

Scheduled to compete in the tournament were: the Bacons, Miller's and Debonairs of Cleveland; Peerless and Peps of Chattanooga; Riceville, Lupton City and the Etowah Questionnaires.

The tournament was to begin on March 1. That day, the *Chattanooga Daily Times*, reported that, "A.A.U. rules barred Jackie Mitchell, pro baseball player, who was to have played with the Peps." The very next day a different picture of the tournament began to emerge. The *Daily Times* reported that the tourney organizers, had "arranged their rules to prevent one very strong club and another with drawing power, both from Chattanooga, from taking part."

R.J. Schlueter, manager of Mitchell's team, the Full-Vues, stated that the announcement that the tourney was to be played under A.A.U. rules was, "misleading, since the teams competing are not members of the A.A.U." and that his team "had played the Bacon club twice during the season." According to Schlueter, "Cliff Campbell, who is running the meet, is in possession of a bid from the A.A.U. for the Bacon team to take part in the national meet in Wichita. Campbell told him that Miss Mitchell could not compete and that he would have to leave her off and call his team the Peps." Campbell later told Schlueter that, "He could not even play the girls who were on the same team with Jackie."

The other Chattanooga club left out of the tourney were the Erlanger Nurses, coached by Nan Elberfeld. The Erlanger team has beaten the Bacon club during the season.

W.C. Campbell, manager of the Charles H. Bacon team, refuted much of Schlueter's version of the story in the *Chattanooga Daily Times* on March 3. Bacon denied that," he is individually running the tourney" and that "Mitchell had not been barred on the account of being a professional." Campbell said that Schlueter is the one who, "raised the question as to Jackie Mitchell's eligibility to participate in such a meet. He (Schlueter) said that Mitchell was a professional and would not be eligible." Campbell went on to say that he told Schlueter, "to pick his players and enter whatever team he might choose. That was the last we heard from Schlueter. In fact, the officials waited for three-quarters of an hour last night for Mr. Schlueter to appear with his team for their game. If Mr. Schlueter was forced to abandon his plans for entering a team, it was for reasons other than rulings made by officials of the tourney."

Campbell went on to note that the Erlanger team was left out of the tourney because they had not turned their paperwork in on time.

CHAPTER 8
Jackie and Babe (Didrikson)

Beginning in February, Jackie Mitchell's manager R. J. Schlueter already started to develop her schedule for the 1933 baseball season. On February 13, a *Chattanooga Daily Times* story headline announced, "Miss Mitchell To Hurl For Orioles In Florida."

The was big news as the Orioles were members of the International Baseball League. According to her manager, the appearance would take place on March 20 in Jacksonville, Florida. Schlueter said that he has received a letter from Percy Dawson, the Orioles business manager asking for Jackie's appearance at Jacksonville. According to the letter, the plan would be to use Jackie in the first exhibition game after the Orioles return to Baltimore from their training camp."

However, the next opportunity for Jackie that the newspapers picked up on would dwarf the Orioles story.

A *Chattanooga Daily Times* story on March 9 was headlined with, "Jackie Mitchell Challenges Babe Didrikson To Face Her On Slab This Summer." Back in March of 1931, prior to her facing Babe Ruth and Lou Gehrig, Jackie had been with a Chattanooga basketball team that was competing in an A.A.U. women's tournament. Didrikson was also playing with a team at that tournament, so at the very least there was the possibility the two of them had met.

By 1932, Didrikson was one of the most recognizable athletes of the time following her performance in the Olympics that year. Didrikson's nickname of "Babe" was given to her because as a young girl, she hit a baseball like Babe Ruth, while Jackie Mitchell's strikeout of Ruth and Lou Gehrig made her equally recognizable.

This idea may have been the work of Jackie's manager who was looking to capitalize on the success of these two athletes. Schlueter in the article stated, "Jackie will pitch against her anywhere suitable to Miss Didrikson, with any teams competing which Miss Didrikson desires. We prefer Yankee Stadium. That can be worked out between Miss Didrikson's manager and myself when the challenge is accepted."

This was not the first time in history that one female athlete challenged another to go head to head. In a similar baseball story nearly a generation earlier, women's baseball pioneer Maud Nelson was challenged by Alta Weiss to meet in a mound duel. It was a match-up which would never take place.

The story would go on to highlight the national appearances that Jackie had made, how many miles she had traveled in her playing career as well as mentioning a crowd she pitched before in 1931 which numbered some 7,500.

Schlueter stated that, "Jackie is booked in Reading and Baltimore, but that efforts will be made to stage the game in any city suitable to the Babe."

The wait for a response for Didrikson did not take long. Later that same day according to an Associated Press story from Dallas, Texas, Babe did not sound particularly happy about the challenge.

Didrikson said, "If I were to accept every challenge that came to me, I'd work my fool head off. Why, I'd be busy every hour of the day and night filling engagements that really don't mean anything." She would go on to add, " My answer is that I don't accept challenges like that, but, if I ever happen to be anywhere at the same time as Jackie is there, I'll let her see whether she an out-pitch me and bet she can't."

Most of the time after a back and forth exchange between athletes on something like a challenge, most of the chatter would just fade away. However, this story still had something left to it.

One day after Didrikson's response, *Chattanooga Daily Times* sports columnist, Wirt Gammon, had some observations to share in his "Sports Parade" column. Gammon said, "(Chattanooga Lookouts owner) Joe Engel claims that Babe Didrikson is merely trying to avoid meeting Jackie Mitchell on the mound and that such a match would mean more to the Babe financially than those billiards and basketball games." He went on to add, "Jackie's publicity did not go to her head. She's the same Jackie she was. I don't know Miss Didrikson personally, but I do know that Jackie, if in Babe's shoes would never have popped off like the Babe did."

Later that month, Schlueter and Engel were not ready to let the story go either. A *Chattanooga Daily Times* story announced, "Engel To Arrange For Jackie, Babe To Meet In Game." The story said that Engel was promising to arrange a pitching battle between Mitchell and Didrikson in a southern league park. Schlueter stated that, he has "opened negotiations with the Dallas club of the Texas League to have the mound duel in Babe's home city. If those fall through, he would then call on Engel. The two girl hurlers would probably be brought together in New Orleans." Schlueter went on to add, "Jackie is working out daily under the training of Lester Vann and is pitching better than ever. She has also added weight since last fall and throws a faster ball."

To help in her travels during the upcoming season, Jackie received a brand new Ford automobile from the D.S. Etheridge company, a local Ford and Lincoln distributor in Chattanooga. A March 19 photograph in the *Chattanooga Daily Times* shows Mitchell receiving the car from sales manager, Forest Cate. Jackie says that she will use the care on her trips during the coming baseball season and she likes the Ford because of its reliability and economy. The tire cover will carry the slogan: "This Ford is from Chattanooga – the Dynamo of Dixie –To live there is a pleasure."

While the exchanges back and forth regarding the challenge played out in the newspapers, another story crept into the pages of the *Chattanooga Daily Times*. On March 20, a headline read, "Jackie Mitchell Has Rival In Ann McNally." According to the story, a 14-year old girl named Ann McNally who was from Chickamauga, Georgia, had enrolled in Kid Elberfeld's baseball school in Atlanta. Like Jackie, she was also a lefthanded pitcher. Elberfeld stated, "Miss McNally is a more promising prospect than was Miss Mitchell." The story went on to add that Ann, "looks forward to a professional career on the mound."

Schlueter was also working on a way to fund Jackie's baseball tour for the upcoming season. Two local businessmen from Chattanooga, Squire Wilkes T. Thrasher and Dr. J.C. Eldridge would "sponsor a committee to raise money for the tour this summer, from civic pride and a desire to advertise Chattanooga," according to Schlueter. He went on to add that Jackie's tour would begin about April 10 or 12 when she would play in the Middle Atlantic and New York-Pennsylvania Leagues, followed by pitching for the Orioles in Florida before going on to New York for additional exhibition games. Schlueter also indicated in another short news article that, "Mitchell is seeking a game at the World's Fair in Chicago, adding that *Photoplay* magazine may assist her in getting the opportunity of performing."

In early April, the challenge story appeared to come to a conclusion. It appeared that Didrikson had backed off her earlier statement and would be willing to accept a challenge from Mitchell. According to an April 7 story in the *Chattanooga Daily Times*, "Babe Didrikson has accepted Jackie Mitchell's challenge to pitch against her this summer and the Boston Red Sox are seeking to sign Miss Mitchell," according to Schlueter. He went on to say, "Miss Didrikson accepted the challenge of Miss Mitchell, saying that she would meet Jackie any time suitable to both parties and that Miss Didrikson talked very pleasantly and is delight to have the chance to meet Jackie."

According to Schlueter, the location for the game had not yet been set and until further in the season as he was trying to get cities to bid for the planned game. As for the Red Sox interest in Mitchell, Schlueter said, "Negotiations are underway for the purchase by the Boston Red Sox of Miss Jackie Mitchell from the Chattanooga club. Eddie Collins, manager of the Red Sox, has expressed a willingness to purchase this star southpaw."

Later on that same evening, Engle, Mitchell and Schlueter were guests of the Middle Tennessee Club. Schlueter was hoping to present a proposition to the club to honor Jackie. He said that Engel would "point out that the value of having Miss Mitchell represent the city of Chattanooga in an advertising campaign and civic pride."

During this entire exchange on the Mitchell and Didrikson "challenge", it seems that everyone was weighing in with a comment. Local sportswriters, Lookouts owner Joe Engel (who originally signed Jackie); R. J. Schlueter (Jackie's business manager) and Babe Didrikson herself. The lone voice that never seemed to be quoted in any story, was that of Jackie Mitchell.

CHAPTER 9
Barnstorming with The House of David

Plans for Jackie's 1933 season were starting to take shape in the early part of May. According to a May 3 mention in the *Chattanooga Daily Times*, her manager said that she would "open up in the Middle Atlantic League" within three or four days.

Another week went by before a more definitive slate was announced in the *Chattanooga Daily Times* on May 11. In that article, Schlueter stated that Jackie, "Would leave tomorrow on a lengthy exhibition tour and is booked for ten exhibition games in the Carolinas and will make a stop at Richmond, Virginia." He also noted that she would open a series of International League games at Baltimore and late in the summer, Jackie would pitch in Chicago. Mitchel was quoted as saying that," Morisse Mudge of *Photoplay* magazine would sponsor her work around the Windy City."

The story also said Jackie hoped to pitch in some major league exhibition games and would close her tour around September 10 in the Texas League and that she planned to oppose Babe Didrikson in a game at Dallas.

According to the story, Jackie had trained for two months and is stronger than before and would be ready to pitch three to five innings, three or four times a week. The story went on to say that Jackie's records have her pitching 100 games against mens' clubs and she has been the winning pitcher in over half of those.

Schlueter also noted a change in what Jackie would wear for her appearances. A special baseball uniform with "Chattanooga" across the front would be worn by her when she pitched.

On May 28, Jackie hurled her first game of the season for the Ironton team of the E.K. League in Ohio. There was no game result posted, but Jackie was credited with starting the game and pitching the first two innings.

In many towns where Jackie would play, the local sportswriters would often offer commentary on her play in their columns. On May 30, a sports column in the *Bluefield Daily Telegraph* carried an interesting note of Jackie. In the "Fodder For Sports From The Press Box" talked about Jackie's strikeout of Ruth and Gehrig and said that she, "is on a tour and trying to lay up some jack by making personal appearances in the various towns." The column goes on to say, "The girl's press agent says she started this season with a Mississippi Valley League team and pitched a three-hit game but decided to quit organized ball for barnstorming."

On June 1, the *Chattanooga Daily Times* carried a short wire story from Huntington, West Virginia. The story said that about 2,000 fans had seen Jackie hurl a 2-1 win in a Middle Atlantic League game on the day before. The short mention is not clear if this was an exhibition or as was stated, an actual league game. A check of the May 31 games in the Middle Atlantic League show that the Beckley Black Knights edged Zanesville by a score of 2-1. It was the only game that day ending with that score. The game account does not list Mitchell in the linescore, nor does it mention any appearance by her that day in an exhibition.

Her next outing would be in the Middle Atlantic League, on June 3 pitching for the Beckley Black Knights against the Dayton Ducks. In a feature story on Jackie before the game, the June 2, *Beckley Post Herald* said, "Jackie is carried on the suspended list of the Lookouts and for the past few years has been going the rounds of baseball parks in the Southland exhibiting her pitching wares to crowded parks at each appearance."

Her appearance with Beckley was an exhibition. Jackie started and pitched three innings, giving up three runs, getting a 5-3 "win." The exhibition was similar to those that she pitched last year in the Piedmont League.

The very next day, Jackie was back on the hill. This time, she pitched for the Welch Senators against the Bishop Miners. Mitchell started the game, pitched the first three innings, giving up but one hit. Although not the pitcher of record, the Senators won the game by a score of 5-1.

Following her stopover in the Middle Atlantic League, Jackie would be back on the road for her next appearance. This time she would showcase her pitching in the New York-Pennsylvania League.

On June 12, Jackie was slated to take the hill in an afternoon game at Island Park for the Harrisburg Senators in an afternoon tilt against the Reading Red Sox at Island Park. Jackie's appearance would be an exhibition game which would take place right before the regular contest. However, the next day, wet grounds forced the postponement of the exhibition and scheduled game.

A couple of weeks later, Jackie would be looking to pitch in her fourth game of the season as she would start for Hopewell in their Central Jersey League contest against Flemington on June 25.

On July 11, 1933, Jackie Mitchell signed a contract with the House of David Eastern team. The contract would pay her a monthly salary of $1,000 In this photograph, Jackie shows her curveball pitching grip to teammates Harry Laufer (center) and George Anderson. (Source: Diamond Dreams Collection)

Jackie got the start that day and hurled the first three innings. She allowed three runs and gave a base on balls in her stint as Hopewell finished on top by a score of 13-7. The *Trenton Evening Times*, said, "Miss Mitchell, a southern sidewinder with unusually good control for a girl, gained herself plenty of admirers in pitching three innings."

Mitchell was followed to the mound by Jim Duffy who was referred to be the newspaper as a "235 pound clown who was almost as broad as he is long." Taking the hill from Mitchell, Duffy during his six innings on the mound, "threw to first base behind his back, flipped the ball to a batter while winding up, played for part of the game without a glove and raced a runner to first base to make the last out of the game."

While in New Jersey, the next part of Jackie Mitchell's baseball story was about to unfold.

On July 1, The House of David's Eastern touring team was in the same area as Mitchell.

The House of David was a religious community founded in Benton Harbor, Michigan in 1903 by Benjamin Purnell. Baseball was first played by the community in 1913. Purnell, a sports enthusiast, would eventually use a barnstorming baseball program to help raise funds for the community as well as recruiting new potential members. A unique feature about the club is that all of their players wore beards, as they were not allowed to cut their hair or shave their beards. If they picked up players who did not join the community, they either had to grow or wear a fake beard.

The House of David began their baseball barnstorming in 1920 and would eventually have two traveling clubs, an Eastern and a Central team.

That day, they would be taking on the Trenton Cadets of the Central Jersey League, the same team that Jackie would pitch for on July 2.

The local Trenton club would come out on the short end of a 10-3 score in the July 1 game against the House of David. The next day, Jackie Mitchell started on the mound for the Trenton Cadets as they took on Chester. Mitchell would hurl three innings, surrendering three runs while stringing out one and giving up one walk.

However, the Trenton roster that day not only featured Mitchell, but also Agnes "Ginger" Robinson who would play second base. Living in nearby Morrisville, New Jersey, Robinson was well-known in the world of baseball. Only 21 years old, she had already played for two noted all-female baseball teams, including the Philadelphia Bobbies and New York Bloomer Girls.

Despite their unique connection as female baseball players, Robinson was not impressed by Mitchell. The two had met on the diamond in May of 1931 when Robinson, then with the New York Bloomer Girls, came to play Mitchell's Junior Lookout team in Chattanooga. "She's not so hot," said Robinson in a July 6, *Trenton Evening Times* story. "We knocked her out of the box in spite of the fact that she had men to support her," she would go on to add.

However, Robinson's memory and the facts from the May, 1931 are vastly different. In the game against the New York Bloomer Girls, Jackie started, threw three shutout innings and surrendered no hits in a 7-4 Junior Lookout win over the Bloomer Girls.

On July 8, the *Trenton Evening Times* reported that, "Schlueter and Miss Mitchell came to the parting of ways this week, when Dr. Joseph S. Mitchell, Chattanooga optician and father of Jackie, objected to Schlueter's method of handling the finances." In that same article, it was reported that Schlueter had substituted, "Miss Agnes (Ginger) Robinson of Morrisville (New Jersey), for the celebrated Miss Jackie Mitchell for his present tour of this section." The day before, *Chattanooga Daily Times* sports Columnist, Wirt Gammon, had already noted, "R.J. Schlueter has resigned as Jackie's manager."

In early July, a number of newspapers published a photograph of a nicely dressed Jackie Mitchell, showing off her pitching grip to St. Louis Cardinals pitcher, Dazzy Vance. When young Jackie lived in Memphis, Vance, a pitcher for the local minor league team, reportedly worked with her on her pitching skills. However, the descriptive cutline of this 1933 photograph, does not reference their prior connection and gives the impression that they are meeting for the first time.

It did not take long for Jackie to find herself with a new baseball opportunity, following her split with former manager Schlueter. On July 11, the *Muscatine Journal* of Iowa, announced that Ray L. Doan, business manager for the House of David baseball clubs, has just signed Jackie Mitchell to pitch for the Eastern House of David team. Jackie was signed for a salary of $1,000 month. She would join the team immediately in Middletown, New York and be with them through the end of their season in the middle of September. Jackie, unlike other players who would join the team, would not have to don a fake beard. For the first time since the Junior Lookouts days, Jackie would have a team that she would be a part of, instead of the solo appearances Jackie made over the past couple of years. Also, negotiating a fee or percentage of gate receipts she would receive would not have to be done with the security of a House of David contract.

Jackie's father Joseph took over the role of serving as her agent after the family parted ways with Schlueter. Prior to signing with the House of David, Jackie's father said that she earned between $300-400 in 1932 for her pitching work.

Managing the Eastern team was Charles "Chief" Bender, former star pitcher with the Philadelphia Athletics of the American League. Bender won over 200 games for a number of major league teams and eventually would be selected to the Baseball Hall of Fame in 1953.

According to the *Middletown Times Herald*, Bender was excited to add Mitchell to his club. In a July 17 story, Bender stated that, "Many fans feel that by using a girl flinger the zip and thrill of a real ball contest will be dulled, but they're mistaken inasmuch as Miss Mitchell is by no means a girl insofar as her expertness is concerned." He would go on to add, "I class her with the best men flingers this club has ever used. And that's a promise. Not only because she's a girl but because she can win ball games is she worth that much dough to us."

On July 17, Jackie took to the mound for the House of David in a night game against the Brown Hunter's Grays. The House of David teams traveled with a portable lighting system that allowed them to play night games. Her opposing pitcher that night was a 17-year old high school pitcher by the name of Billy Stahlin. According to the *Times Herald,* Mitchell was "decidedly, ineffective – stagestruck," according to those who had seen her pitch before. It was noted that she had a hard time "controlling her slow dropping curve, even after an unusually long warm-up." Jackie tossed but a single inning but was not scored upon in the eventual House of David, 2-1 loss before a crowd of over 2,500.

Following her first start, a story appeared in the *Omaha World Herald* (Nebraska) on July 18. In a column titled, "Women's World It Seems" author Lemuel F. Parton, related a story of Jackie when she was a young girl.

"When Jackie was a little girl, Jackie's father saw her heave a rock with such speed and accuracy that he got Dazzy Vance to coach her. She was a sensation on the sandlots, but nevertheless postponed her pitching career while she attended Signal School, a private preparatory school for girls. She is a snub-nosed, blue-eyed, ingenuous girl with flat brown hair and medium figure. Her windup is like cranking a model T, but she is said to get a puzzling kink on the ball. She was a sickly child, and the coaching regime was, like Theodore Roosevelt's, prescribed as a curative."

The next day, Jackie would again get a start for the House of David, this time against the Milton Bradley team of Springfield, Massachusetts. Again, under the lights and before a crowd of nearly 3,000 fans, Jackie hurled in opening inning, surrendering a pair of hits, a walk and one run. Her club would rally and would eventually to their hosts by a score of 4-2.

Extraordinary Attraction!
NIGHT BASEBALL
BETWEEN
HOUSE of DAVID
Central and Eastern States Teams
Saturday, August 26, at 8:30 P. M.
at
Eden Springs
Featuring Miss Jackie Mitchell, girl wonder pitcher
Park Illuminated by special $30,000 lighting plant

Near the end of the 1933 baseball season, the Eastern and Central House of David teams would meet to play a game at their home local at Eden Park in Benton Harbor, Michigan. This advertisement for the game, highlighted both Jackie's appearance and the lighting system at the field. (Source: News-Palladium, *August 24, 1933)*

Working a second straight day, Mitchell would start and toss one inning, giving up walk and strike out one batter versus the Greenfield Mohawks (New York) in a 3-1 win. Before the month of July would end, the House of David would play a scheduled doubleheader in the towns of Wooster and Brockton, Massachusetts.

Jackie would start the games in Wooster and Brockton. Newspaper reports credit her with a scoreless inning in the game against Wooster. The House of David lost a 3-2 decision to Wooster, but would scored a 9-3 victory over Taunton Lumber at Brockton with Jackie tossing the first inning.

In an August 2 start against the Mercury ball-club in Vermont, Jackie would allow one hit and was not the pitcher of decision in a 5-3 House of David victory. Pitching before over 3,500 fans against Guy's Ball Club in Plattsburgh, New York, Jackie would have a rough start, surrendering two hits and two walks in her inning of work. However, the House of David would win the game by a score of 5-4 in 13 innings. Two days later Jackie would throw a scoreless inning in relief against the Canton (New York) Pirates in a 13-2 win.

Another large crowd came out to see Jackie and her team take on a strong club from Oswego (New York). In the first night game played at their field, a standing room only crowd of over 2,200 fans, saw the hometown club tag a 5-0 on Jackie and the House of David. Jackie for her part, started the game and surrendered a first inning run on four hits before being taken from the mound at the end of the inning. It was Jackie's first loss since September 10, 1932, when she was on the mound for the Norfolk Orioles.

Rain threated the Jackie's August 8 start against a Syracuse, New York club, the Byrne-Seiberlings. Before a crowd of 1,000, she tossed one complete inning and did not allow a hit, walk or run as her team triumphed by a score of 13-5 in a five inning contest.

In her next games, Jackie would pitch against two minor league teams from the New York-Pennsylvania League. On August 12, she started against the Elmira Redwings (New York). According to the August 13, *Elmira Advertiser*, Jackie started the game and was touched up for four hits and three runs. The House of David however, saved her from a loss as they rallied to top Elmira by a score of 7-4.

Moving into Pennsylvania, she would fair better, throwing a scoreless first inning against the Wilkes-Barre Barons, another New York-Pennsylvania minor league club. Before a crowd of more than 4,000. Jackie would allow one hit, and no runs and struck out a batter before leaving the game after the first inning due to an injured finger. She would miss one more game in Pennsylvania as she was suffering from tonsillitis.

On August 17, Jackie faced a local all-star team from Huntingdon Before over 3,000 fans, she would get the start, toss a scoreless inning allowing but a walk as the House of David won by a score of 4-0. Her last opponent in Pennsylvania was a local team from Somerset. Jackie would start and throw the first inning as her club would win by a score of 20-3. The game drew a crowd of 1,500.

As the House of David moved into Ohio, Jackie would first face the Zieglers of Canton on August 20. She would start the game as the first three hitters all went out on groundouts. That was her only inning of work as her club came out on top by a score of 3-1. Working a second straight day, Jackie would face the Westinghouse Electrics. In her lone inning of work as a starter, Jackie was touched up for three hits and three runs in an 11-7 House of David victory. Starting for the third consecutive day, Jackie would take to the mound against the Carey Semi-Pros. The box score does not indicate how many innings she pitched that day, but the House of David would win the game by a score of 12-2.

The next opponent for the House of David was the strong Skrzycki team from Detroit, Michigan. In the past several seasons, the Skrzycki club had played 100 games according to the local newspapers and had lost but three during that time. Former Detroit Tiger star, Harry Heilman was going to serve as honorary manager for the August 23 tilt. Heilman hoped to play an inning or two against the House of David, anticipating an at bat against the lefthanded Mitchell.

"Maybe she can strike me out," said Heilman in an August 23 story in the *Detroit Times*. "To be honest, I doubt it. I know she can pitch with either hand and that she has what ball players call plenty of stuff on the ball, but I still believe I can connect," he went on to add.

He also noted that should he strike out, he would rank himself as one of three great batters of all times who have fanned before the blue-eyed

Jackie and that twice she fanned Babe Ruth. Once when the umpire called him out and the second time when he took one of his famous swings.

The game was played at Navin Field, home of the major league Detroit Tigers. Built in 1912, it would later be known as Briggs Stadium and finally, Tiger Stadium and would be home to the Tigers from 1912-1999. The House of David-Skrzycki game would be the first night game played at the field.

A crowd of 15,000 was on hand to see Jackie Mitchell on the mound for this first historic night game. Pitching a fourth day in a row, her outing however was a short one. She started the game and pitched to four hitters. The first two were easy outs, but the third batter was walked. The fourth batter hit a grounder to first and as Mitchell went to cover the base, she collided with Skrzycki's Nick Shenk. That collision allowed the ball to roll free and the runner to score. Shaken up on the play, Jackie would leave the game. Her teammates would come back to take a lead in the game, but would eventually drop the contest by a score of 5-4.

The day after the game, the *Detroit Times*, ran another feature story on Jackie. Like many stories beforehand, it mentioned the tie the Mitchell family had to Dazzy Vance and talked about how Vance "predicted that she would be a great ballplayer." The story also said that her father was currently serving as her coach and manager and that he had played minor league baseball 20 years ago. At the time the story was written, the reporter noted that, "Miss Mitchell had been with the bearded team in its last 45 games and had hurled in 41 of them and has only one defeat. Her batting average is envied by many stars and included among her hits are eight home runs."

Jackie recovered from her collision at first quickly and was back on the mound for a fifth day in a row, this time to face the Battle Creek (Michigan) Postums. She would again get the start and, before a crowd numbering 5,000 and did not give up a hit, walk or run in her outing.

On August 26, Mitchell's former manager R.J. Schlueter was in the news in his hometown of Richmond, Virginia. The *Times-Dispatch* reported, "The House of David had signed his protégé to replace the injured Chief Bender." Schlueter also noted, "She is now looking forward to a contest with Babe Didrikson and a vaudeville tour this winter. She is a southpaw knuckleball pitcher and calls herself the woman's auxiliary of the House of David."

As the month of August was drawing to a close, the Eastern and Central House of David teams were back in Benton Harbor and would face

During the winter of 1933-34, Jackie joined Babe Didrikson's All-Americans basketball club. Both Jackie and Babe met in Dallas during the March, 1931 AAU basketball tournament. Over the course of their athletic careers, they had a friendly rivalry. This was the first time however, that they were able to be teammates. From left to right are: Jackie Mitchell, Babe Didrikson and Gladys Crossly. (Source: Chattanooga Daily Times, *December 3, 1933)*

each other at Eden Park on August 27. Some 1,500 fans were on hand that night to see the Central team easily handle the Eastern club by a score of 10-3. Although she did not start, the fans got to see Jackie enter the game with one out in the eighth inning and a runner on base. She got the first hitter to ground out and struck out the next batter to end the inning.

After the stopover in Benton Harbor, Jackie and her club went back on the road. Her first outing would be against the minor league American Association's Saint Paul Saints on September 4. As had been the case for Jackie most of the year, she started the game and pitched the first inning. Although she gave up a pair of hits, she did not surrender a run in her outing as the House of David would go on to win by a score of 11-3. A new article in the *Chattanooga Daily Times* mentioned, "Babe Didrikson, a Texas girl athlete saw the game and again challenged her to a pitcher's duel."

Several days later, Jackie would miss a game versus a team from Hurley, Wisconsin due to an infected tooth.

Feature articles about Jackie continued to appear in newspapers all over the country. On September 8, the *Centralia Evening Sentinel* (Illinois) reported on her time with the House of David, prior to her upcoming appearance against the St. Louis Cardinals. "Miss Jackie Mitchell, a 19-year old girl blonde southpaw, is the only member of the House of David who doesn't wear whiskers. And oddly enough her hair is shorter than most of the male members of the team."

A short news story from Norfolk, Virgina that appeared in the September 9, *Chattanooga Daily Times*, reported, "Jackie Mitchell, Chattanooga's girl pitcher, may enter the movies. She is expected to sign a contract here, with a producer whose name is not divulged, to play in a baseball picture."

On September 12, perhaps the biggest game of the year would take place for Jackie's team. The major league St. Louis Cardinals were the slated opposition as they hosted the House of David nine. In perhaps her most important appearance since 1931 when she faced the New York Yankees, Mitchell was the starting pitcher against another big league club.

Before a crowd of over 10,000 under the lights at Sportsman Park, Mitchell got the starting nod. Lead-off hitter Pepper Martin grounded out, but the second batter outfield George Watkins, hit a single to bring the third place hitter, Frankie Frisch to the plate.

Mitchell got the best of their match-up as she forced Frisch to hit into an inning ending double play to keep the Cardinals scoreless. Her team would go on to defeat the National League team by a score of 8-6.

Later stories about Mitchell's appearance against the Cardinals would talk about her success, including a strikeout of Hall of Famer Leo Durocher. However, Durocher never batted against Mitchell. Their lone connection was Jackie's only at bat against the major league team, when she hit a pop-up to Durocher who was playing shortstop that day.

The House of David would next look to take on the Kansas City Monarchs on September 19. That day, anticipating her appearance, the *Kansas City Star* mentioned that "Shoeless" Joe Jackson had watched her pitch and was convinced. "I never thought I'd live to see a girl pitch that well," commented Jackson. However, due to an unspecified injury, Mitchell would miss a game against the Kansas City Monarchs. The very next day she would face the LaCrosse Troubadours (Wisconsin). Perhaps still not quite up to par, Mitchell got her start, but would give up three hits and a pair of runs in her lone inning of work. Oddly enough, the game was called with a 5-5 score because of darkness. Since the game was not slated to be a night game, the portable lights used by the Eastern House of David were not used.

With the 1933 baseball season at an end, the *Chattanooga Daily Times*, gave a summary of Jackie's season in an article on October 10. According to the story, Jackie had "hurled in 65 contests this past summer for the Benton Harbor nine and only allowed 21 runs to cross the plate." The story went on to add that she "drew 125,000 fans through the turnstiles, including 15,000 in Detroit and 10,000 in St. Louis and that she had been offered another contract for next season."

As the baseball season wound down, the planned World's Fair appearance and pitching match-up against Babe Didrikson did not materialize. Jackie would now turn her attention to basketball as well as her preparation for the 1934 baseball season.

In that same October 10 article, another potential meeting of Jackie Mitchell and Babe Didrikson was talked about. However, this new mention was not about meeting on the baseball field rather, the story mentioned that the two, "may play on the same basket ball quintet this winter, as Jackie has been offered a contract on the Babe's team, but no satisfactory financial agreement has been reached as yet."

Over the next month, there was also some discussion in the newspapers that Jackie might join a male professional team from Chattanooga. An early workout for the club was held at the City High gym and was attended by the team Captain, Jude Baesman, along with "Bill Redd, Babe Mitchell, Paul Roy and Houghton, a newcomer."

On November 14, *Chattanooga Daily Times* sportswriter Wirt Gammon, reported that, "Jackie Mitchell has been offered $10,000 to pitch five months next season." The mention of the contract appeared in Gammons' "Sports Parade" column, but does not detail who made the offer to Jackie.

Just two days later came the announcement that indeed, "Jackie Mitchell, that great little girl athlete and baseball hurler" would be joining Babe Didrikson's All-Americans basketball quintet, according to Ray L. Doan, the team business manager. The *Muscatine Journal And News Tribune*, reported hat Jackie had stated that she was chosen an All-American forward in a girls' independent basketball tournament at Dallas, Tex., three years ago. In that tournament she played against Miss Didrikson."

According to Doan, team members would report to train in Muscatine, Iowa on November 22 for 10 days, including several preseason games to be played against the Muscatine Junior College quintet and Olson's Terrible Swedes.

Besides, Didrikson and Mitchell, the rest of the team included Darrall Darby (former University of Kentucky star); "Lefty" Beyers, (Kansas State); Carl Howard and Dick Butzen (Loyola of Chicago) and Bob Gruening (Northwestern University).

The season was not going to turn out to be a good one for Jackie. Early on, as scores for the All-Americans began to show up in newspapers, so did the reports of Jackie suffering from injuries. During the teams' first month of play, she is mentioned as being part of the club, yet either plays very little or not at all. When the All-Americans were in Denver on December 11, the *Denver Post* reported, She (Jackie) has left the club leaving Miss Didrikson as the only woman player."

The very next day, the *Chattanooga Daily Times* stated, "Jackie Mitchell, member of Babe Didrikson's All-American basketball team, has returned home to recover from injuries suffered in a game. A toe injury has healed, but a side bruise will keep her inactive until December 20, when

In the spring of 1934, Jackie Mitchell was a holdout to sign her contact with the House of David. They had offered her the same contract as 1933 ($1,000 per month). When Jackie chose not to re-up with the team, The House of David signed Mildred "Babe" Didrikson to a $1,000 a month contract to pitch for the Eastern team. Babe is pictured here with teammates Bob (center) and Tom Dewhirst. (Source: Diamond Dreams Collection)

she will rejoin her team at Chicago. It was a reunion which would never happen.

By January, Jackie was back on the local hardwood in Chattanooga. She had just recently joined the Standard team In a January 13 match-up against the Peerless team, Jackie's club fell by a score of 52-5. She was listed a center for her team and scored one point.

CHAPTER 10
On Her Own Once More

Near the end of the 1933 baseball season, the House of David had expressed to Jackie that they were interested in bringing her back for the next season. In early March, the team offered to bring back Jackie in 1934 at the same $1,000 per month salary she received the previous season.

According to a *Chattanooga Daily Times* report on April 6, Jackie had "spurned an offer of her last year's salary." The story added, "Jackie has until June 1 when the club starts training to come to terms, it is understood, and will be affiliated this season the western division, while Grover Cleveland Alexander shifts over to the eastern team." While in preparation for the 1934 season, the April 12, *Daily Times* reported that Jackie was a special guest of Chattanooga's Troop 8 Boy Scouts at a recent meeting.

About 10 days after reporting that Jackie had rejected a contract based on her 1933 terms, the House of David did sign a female pitcher for the 1934 season. Mildred "Babe" Didrikson, however, was making pitching appearances at major league spring training camps. Based on her appearances, The House of David would ink her to a contract of $1,000 per month. She would play for the Eastern House of David Team under manager Grover Cleveland Alexander. Her signing however, still left the door open for Jackie to re-sign for 1934.

The rest of the spring is a quiet one for Jackie. In Wirt Gammons' "Just Between Us Fans" *Chattanooga Daily Times* sports column on May 12, he notes that Jackie was planning "an extensive baseball tour" and that, "She will not be with the House of David," and it is not until early June when news comes out about her plans for the season.

The June 8, *Chattanooga Daily Times*, reported that Jackie would soon begin her annual pitching tour. According to the story, "The girl southpaw will move on Cincinnati, Boston and New York, meeting Mid-Atlantic and Northeastern League teams and many semipro clubs en route."

On June 29, Jackie was signed to make a pitching appearance in Xenia, Ohio. Two teams were being recruited from Central High School for the game and Jackie would be slated to hurl two or three innings for one of the clubs.

Before the game started however, Xenia school officials had a concern about whether or not admission could be charged for the exhibition, especially since Mitchell would be pitching for one of the teams and she did hold a professional contract. The local fear was by charging admission, it would invalidate the eligibility of the high school players to play as amateurs.

When officials tried to contact H.R. Townsend, commissioner of the Ohio High School Athletic Association, he could not be reached. According to the *Xenia Evening Gazette*, "The officials decided to play it safe. It was agreed that admission at the gate would not be charged, but that the hat would be passed and a collection taken among the fans. That method they felt, would solve the problem and not injure the amateur status of the high school boys." Mitchell did start and toss two exhibition innings, but no other details about the game were reported.

In a follow-up story on Mitchell following her local appearance, the "Sport Snap Shots" column in the *Xenia Evening Gazette* spoke to Jackie's manager about her upcoming activities. Although the manager is not named in the story, it's possible that Maltier Chauncey is being interviewed by the writer. Chauncey was from Chattanooga and was the dramatic teacher at Brainerd Junior High School. Her relationship as Jackie's manager would be mentioned in a *Chattanooga Daily Times* story on July 29.

The story notes that "Her (Jackie's) manager says that every place they visit, softball is obtaining a firm foothold and views the increasing popularity of the sport with alarm. Jackie, she confides, also likes to play softball, although pitching baseball is her bread and butter. Jackie's father, however, frowns on the idea of his daughter dividing her time between the two diamond pastimes. He figures the two games don't mix, and that softball might ruin her baseball ability."

Her manager went on to say that she had tried to proposition Larry MacPhail, general manager of the Cincinnati Reds to have Jackie appear at Crosley Field, but he turned her down citing, "He was afraid somebody would make an obvious wisecrack that the Reds are having such a difficult time attracting customers that the management resorted to extraordinary methods by arranging for the appearance of a girl pitcher in order to stimulate gate receipts."

Following her appearance in Xenia, Mitchell would throw two exhibition innings for both the Columbus Red Birds of the American Association and the Zanesville Greys of the Middle Atlantic League. Much as she did in the Piedmont League in 1932, Mitchell would toss exhibition innings for a number of different minor league teams. The only difference from the 1932 appearances is that season she was signed specifically by the league. This season, she booked the appearances with individual clubs.

On July 18, Jackie would start for Harrisburg and toss two exhibition innings against Elmira, giving up but one hit. Several days later, she would face Harrisburg in an appearance with Reading. In that start, she tossed two innings. Both Harrisburg and Reading were members of the New York Penn League. Jackie would hurl one more exhibition game in the New York Penn League. On, July 25, she would play for Hazleton (Pennsylvania) against Harrisburg. She would pitch two innings, surrendering a pair of hits..

While still traveling in the east, Mitchell would get an opportunity to pitch in a non-exhibition setting on July 29. In that game, she started for the Jerseys against a Hoboken team. Jackie would give up a pair of hits and issue one walk, but not surrender a run as her team would top Hoboken by a 9-7 score.

That same day, the *Chattanooga Daily Times* reported that "Jackie Mitchell is bringing Chattanooga plenty of publicity as she exhibits on the mound instead of 'playing' as she formerly did." The story claims that "Chattanooga's feminine offering to the baseball world has smiled from the pages of many periodicals throughout Ohio, New York and Pennsylvania as she endorsed advertisements, ranging from automobiles to the world's highest chair." Her endorsement also included things like jewelry, groceries, paint and sporting goods as well.

The story also noted, "The youthful southpaw has chucked from the pitching hills of six different leagues, the Mid-Atlantic, Piedmont, Cotton

States, Southern, American Association and the New York Pennsylvania." During her travels in the east, the August 1, *Brooklyn Daily Eagle* noted, "Jackie Mitchell, a girl pitcher, will be Exhibit A at Ebbets Field today. It's just a stunt. She may throw in batting practice tomorrow."

A few days after her outing for the Jerseys, Mitchell would take to the mound in an exhibition appearance for the Elmhurst Grays. In a two-inning stint for the Grays against a Trenton, New Jersey team, Mitchell struggled somewhat in her outing, allowing four runs, four hits and one hit by pitch. She would finish with a pair of strikeouts.

Before heading back home, Jackie would sign a contract with the Northeastern League to make appearances with its clubs. An August 11 story in the *Chattanooga Daily Times* reported that Jackie, "was engaged by Roger E. Baker, president of the Northeastern League to debut with the Worcester Rosebuds and then make a tour of the circuit, playing with the other seven clubs."

Mitchell was to debut with the Worcester team on Sunday, August 12 when they faced league opponent Wayland. On a rainy day, some 2,300 fans turned out for the opportunity to see Jackie pitch. However on this day, Jackie missed the first game and did not arrive at the ballpark until the seventh inning of the second game. League president Baker was among those in attendance and decided not to have her pitch an exhibition inning that day. A game account in the *Worcester Evening Gazette* said that Mitchell's late arrival was due to that fact she "was in Harrisburg, Pa., on Saturday and the long trip was retarded somewhat because of an automobile accident en route."

Two days later, Jackie did make her first appearance for a league team, pitching for Springfield against New Bedford. Before about 100 fans and under a new $15,000 lighting system at the Springfield ballpark, Jackie would start and throw a scoreless inning. Afterwards according to the Springfield Republican, "Soon after the exhibition inning, she and her woman manager went into the grandstand and watched the rest of the game."

As August came to an end, Mitchell found herself pitching for the Brownies of Troy, New York, against a local team of All Stars. In a *Troy Times* news article before her August 30 tilt, the paper reported that she was, "the only woman holding a contract recognized by Baseball Commissioner Landis" and, "She is under contract to the Chattanooga club but has been released from her contract to make this exhibition tour." In her outing for the Brownies, Jackie would start and throw the first two innings, giving up a single hit and fanning two. However, her club would come out on the short end of a 6-4 score.

On the September 3 Labor Day holiday, Jackie signed to pitch for three different teams! Two of the teams however, would play each other that day and Jackie would hurl part of a game for each team. In the first game of the day, Mitchell would pitch one inning for Copake's All Stars in their 11-10 loss to West Stockbridge. Game two would find Jackie toss one inning for West Stockbridge against the Copake's All Stars. Although a closer game, West Stockbridge came out on the short end of a 5-3 score in that second game. There is no indication that she was the pitcher of record in either game.

Following the end of that doubleheader, Jackie and her manager drove off for the next game of the holiday schedule. This time she would be slated to pitch in an early evening contest for the Hedricks team of Schenectady against the Gloversville (NY) collegiate team.

There are two different versions of what Jackie did that day. According to the September 4, *Schenectady Daily Gazette*, a traffic accident caused Jackie to arrive late. According to the game report, "She proved her good faith and appeared on the field just after the game was called in the seventh inning and made a hit with the remaining fans by throwing a few curves and speed balls across the plate to Bobby Green." However, another report of that same game from the *Morning Herald* of Gloversville and Johnstown (NY), reported that, "Miss Jackie Mitchell, girl pitcher, hurled a part of an inning against the college outfit last night."

Before heading back to Chattanooga, Mitchell had one more pitching appearance to make. On September 5, Jackie would take to the mound for an exhibition game, this time it would be for the Albany Senators as they played the Baltimore Orioles in an International League contest.

Prior to the start of the game, Jackie would throw two exhibition innings. It would be the fourth documented minor league circuit that she would pitch in during the 1934 season.

Following the end of the 1934 baseball season, Jackie's athletic activities seemed to greatly slow down. Unlike past years, where there is almost a seamless transition from baseball into basketball, the fall and early winter of 1934 were quiet ones for her.

It is not until January 18, when a brief note in the *Chattanooga Daily Times* mentions that Jackie would soon be joining the Clark Bros. Furniture City League girls' basketball team.

The Clark Bros. team would finish in second place in league play. For her part, Jackie would play in five games, three times as a starter and twice off the bench. She would split her time playing either guard or forward. Although she did not score during the season, the highlight was in a February 13 game versus league opponent Samuels. In that 29-5 victory by Clark Bros., Mitchell according to the newspaper, "played great defensive ball, holding her opponent scoreless that night."

The spring and summer were equally as quiet for Jackie. For the first time since she burst onto the Chattanooga baseball scene in 1930 as a member of the Engelettes, there is no indication that Jackie took to the field in 1935.

It's possible that this self-imposed hiatus was due to the fact that she had tired of being on the road. Since 1931, she either traveled as a member of a team or pitched as a solo performer all over the eastern part of the United States for four seasons.

Other than a few mentions in newspaper stories remembering when Jackie had pitched in a community, there were little to no mention of her baseball playing, even in Chattanooga. A March 24 the *Elizabethton Star*, Tennessee newspaper wondered about her, asking, "Where Jackie Mitchell, the great girl baseball pitcher, is laboring now?"

It's not until October of 1935, that the baseball world heard again from Jackie. However, it had nothing to do with her on the field play. Rather, she was offering commentary on a failed appearance in Chattanooga by St. Louis Cardinal pitcher, Dizzy Dean.

On October 17, Dean was to appear at Engel Stadium as part of a game between Peerless and Dixie Spinners baseball teams. The game was to benefit a charity toy fund organized by Chattanooga Lookouts owner, Joe Engel. However that day, a half hour before the game began, there were only 200 spectators in the stands. When Dean saw the showing, he walked out and stated, "I can pick up more money playing poker on the train." Dean objected to going on the field to play, saying, "It is not worth the risk of getting hurt to pitch before that small of a crowd."

It seemed that many people offered commentary on the Dean story and even the shy, reserved Jackie shared her opinion on the issue in the October 19, *Chattanooga Daily Times*. "Jackie Mitchell, Chattanooga Famous Girl Pitcher – 'I think it was a dirty trick. All I have to say is that in my opinion Dizzy Dean is terribly stuck up and thinks he's awful smart. I never in all my life, as long as I have pitched a game of ball, walked out on anybody, and I've pitched over 300 games. I think it was very poor sportsmanship for Dean to walk out the way he did'."

Other than that brief jump into the news, the only other mention of Jackie through the end of the year was on November 25, 1935, when *Chattanooga Daily Times*, sportswriter Wirt Gammons mentioned, "Jackie hopes to join Babe Ruth in his tour to teach English youth baseball and golf," and that she "is brushing up on her golf game now."

Jackie remained out of the spotlight during much of 1936 as well. The only local newspaper mention of Jackie that year was a January 18th trip with her mother to West Palm Beach, Florida, and her attendance at a September 18th linen shower with her sister Josephine. Nationally, Jackie's name would crop up in numerous publications. Most of those were from April of 1936, remembering her strikeouts of Ruth and Gehrig, five years earlier.

CHAPTER 11

One Last Fling: Buck Lai's Hawaiians

After two years away from the baseball diamond, Jackie Mitchell was again on the hunt for baseball playing opportunities. The June 11, 1937, *Chattanooga Daily Times*, reported that she had signed a contract with Kansas City sports promoter, Tom Baird, "for a three months' tour of the United States with the (Buck Lai) Hawaiians."

Jackie joined her new club in Akron, Ohio on June 13 to face the Killian Celtics. The Hawaiians were going to play their season using a portable lighting system previously owned by the House of David, Mitchell's former team. She started the game against the Celtics, allowing two hits, but no runs in her one inning of work. Her good start however did not translate into a win, as the Hawaiians lost by a score of 5-3. The team would then make its way into Pennsylvania.

Her next start was against the Penn Drakes in Titusville. Matching her opening outing for the Hawaiians, Jackie would get the start, allow a pair of hits but no runs and would get a strikeout in her inning of work. The Hawaiians would prevail in the game by a score of 9-8 in 12 innings. On June 23, Jackie started again, this time against the Warren Independents. For the third straight outing, she would give up a pair of hits and no runs in her appearance. The Hawaiians would come up short in the game however, by a score of 8-4.

The very next day, Jackie started again, this time against the Hanley Bricks. The *Bradford Daily Record* gave a glowing assessment of Mitchell's work as a member of the Hawaiians before the game against the locals. "She

THEY'RE COMING TO SAYRE

TUESDAY
AUG. 3

COLEMAN
FIELD
8 P. M.

"Buck" Lai

Hawaiian Baseball Team
FEATURING

"JACKIE" MITCHELL
Girl Pitcher

— VS. —

SAYRE
SHOPS

ADMISSION

40c

In 1937, Jackie returned to the baseball diamond for another season of play. She signed a contract with Buck Lai's Hawaiians. Lai, a former minor leaguer, ran a successful semi-pro team over a number of seasons. Team players would often wear grass skirts on the field as depicted in this 1937 ad. (Source: Evening Times (Sayre, PA), July 28, 1937)

has appeared before thousands of fans since joining the Hawaiians and is smart in baseball ways, has better baseball sense, probably, than the average professional player." The pre-game story went on to say, "She really hasn't got a fastball, but those slow curves, mixed in with a few knuckleballs and a slow one or two, usually do the business when you know where to throw them and are able to throw them there." In this outing versus Hanley, she tossed a scoreless inning, surrendering no hits and finishing with a strike-out as her club won the game by a score of 4-0.

Traveling to Clearfield, Pennsylvania, the Hawaiians would defeat the local club under the lights by a score of 10-2. Hawaiian pitchers surren-dered but two hits in the victory. Jackie would start the game and retire the side in order in her lone inning of work. According to the *Clearfield Prog-ress*, "The first frame did not go down in the record books."

On June 29, the Hawaiians would play the Concordia Singers. In her sixth start of the season, Jackie would throw another scoreless inning for her club, who would come up short on the end of a 3-2 score. After a two-season layoff from playing, Mitchell almost seemed not to miss a beat as she locked down five straight scoreless appearances on the mound.

Still in Pennsylvania in early July, the Hawaiians faced the West Shore All Stars on July 3. Despite Jackie tossing a scoreless first inning, the Ha-waiians would fall by a 4-1 score. The West York Fireman were next on the slate for the Hawaiians. Although Jackie would start and throw the first in-ning, retiring all three hitters, the inning would not count in the final game score, and her appearance would be listed as an exhibition.

Following the game against West York, the Hawaiians traveled to Brooklyn, New York, to play a doubleheader against the Bushwicks. The Hawaiians would drop the opening game by a 4-1 and then lose the night-cap by a 3-1 margin. Jackie would get the start in game two, giving up one hit, no runs and getting two strikeouts. Jackie continued her successful slate, getting another start and scoreless inning in her club's 12-6 win over the Poughkeepsie All-Stars. She followed that appearance up with a one in-ning, scoreless start on July 22 versus the Savitt's Gems in a 9-8 Hawaiians win. The very next day, Jackie got the start against Milton Bradley, tossing one inning and getting no decision in a 5-4 loss.

In her first twelve outings (including the two exhibition games) for the Hawaiians, she tossed twelve scoreless innings, allowing but six hits while striking out three batters. However, despite this success, Jackie still had her detractors. On July 27, the Hawaiians played against the Lowell All-Stars. For the third time during the season, Jackie's inning of work would be con-sidered an exhibition appearance.

Perhaps it was a bit of a letdown for Jackie after her successful start, or maybe it was just an off-night for her. Whatever the case, Jackie would hit the first two batters she faced. It was not clear if she completed her inning or if any runs had scored, as the box score for the game did not include anything since her appearance was considered "exhibition."

It was this outing that became part of a commentary on her skills when *Worcester Evening Gazette* (Massachusetts) reporter Tom Sweeney, gave his opinion of Mitchell in his July 29, "The Sports Trail" column: "Miss Jackie Mitchell, the girl-pitcher, has had fewer runs scored against her than any curver in the land, male or female…But there's a reason…Wherever the Hawaiian All-Stars play, an agreement is made with the opposition that there shall be no scoring in the first inning, and this is the only inning Miss Mitchell pitches…Batters deliberately tap the ball lightly and allow themselves to be retired…Miss Mitchell struck out Babe Ruth once, 'tis said…Afterwards she signed some kind of contract with the Chattanooga Lookouts…As a matter of fact, Miss Mitchell can't pitch a lick right now, and there are girls in this town who can fire the ball at the batter with more speed and form…After looking at her last night, I'm inclined to think that if she ever struck out Ruth it must have been when he wasn't using a bat."

Despite that rather scathing assessment of Jackie's pitching skills, it did not deter her at all for her next appearance on August 2 in Cortland, New York. In a 7-6 Hawaiian club victory, Jackie started the game and tossed a scoreless first inning against the Cobakco team.

The local newspaper reported that, "Jackie Mitchell, the portside girl flinger for the visitors showed her underhand delivery on the mound for the opening inning." While Mitchell's pitching delivery was unique, most images or film from her first couple of seasons, show a lower arm angle that appears to be not quite a sidearm pitching slot. It would not be considered "underhand." It's possible that during the two seasons that Jackie did not play that she might have altered her delivery somewhat. However, if she had, this game report is the only time in all of Mitchell's appearances that her pitching style was noted in that fashion.

On August 3, the Hawaiians would face the Sayre (Pennsylvania) Systems Shop. While Jackie would work in this game, her inning of work at the start of the game was deemed an exhibition inning that would not count in the game record. The Hawaiians would win by the score of 9-7, with the home team committing five errors.

Girl Pitcher Fine Against Oil Nine

Mt. Pleasant—Jackie Mitchell, feminine mound artist, did better than her male successor, Victor Morro, and Buck Lai's Hawaiian team in consequence lost a 4-0 decision to Roosevelt Oils, playing under lights at Island park Wednesday night. Jackie struck out the giant Slim Wilkinson and held the locals hitless in the first inning.

As the 1937 baseball season was coming to an end, this game report may well be the last baseball game appearance by Jackie Mitchell. In a game against the Roosevelt Oil team in Mt. Pleasant, Michigan, Mitchell got the starting nod and retired all three batters that she faced in her inning of work. (Source: Grand Rapids Press,*August 19, 1937*

The next stop for the Hawaiians would be Jamestown, New York. Jackie was again handed the ball to start. Despite giving up a lead-off hit, the next batter hit into a double play and the third batter was retired with no runs being scored. However, the Hawaiians found scoring difficult as well, and they would fall to the Jamestown All-Stars by a 5-0 score.

As the season was winding down for Jackie and the Hawaiians, their next game would mark another notch in Mitchell's baseball record. On August 10, the Hawaiians would square off against minor league opponent, the Mansfield Red Sox, members of the Ohio State League. For Jackie, the game would be considered an exhibition appearance. She would start and toss the opening inning (although not counted in the game record). It would mark the seventh different minor league team that she would either pitch in or against. The Hawaiians would drop this game by a 13-3 score.

The Roosevelt Oil team would be on the slate next for the Hawaiians for an August 18 game in Mt. Pleasant, Michigan. Jackie got the start in that game. According to the *Grand Rapids Press* report of the game the next day, Mitchell, "Struck out the giant Slim Wilkinson and held the locals hitless in the first inning." This may very well have been the final game that Jackie Mitchell pitched in her career. While the Hawaiians would travel to St. Joseph, Michigan for an August 22 game against Joe Green's Chicago Giants, they did so without their female pitcher who, according to the *Herald Press* in St. Joseph, "The Hawaiians, sans the grass skirts they were billed to play in, and without the added attraction of Jackie Mitchell, the girl pitcher whose contract expired two days ago, did manage to display an excellent brand of ball, turning in some spectacular plays."

By August 28, Jackie was back in Chattanooga. An article in the *Chattanooga Daily Times* that day talks about an entertainment program at Fort Oglethorpe, Georgia, in the evening. That entertainment would include, "Chattanooga's only all-girl orchestra, the Rhythmettes, directed by Jessica Elkins. Those in the orchestra are Misses Vivian Gates, Dorothy Case, Beth Thompson, Betty Browne, Fannie Lou Selvidge, Eleanor Boyd and Jackie Mitchell."

CHAPTER 12
Stars of the World

Following the end of her season with the Hawaiians, Jackie would look to transition to basketball. Unlike past seasons when the Chattanooga newspaper would report on her basketball activities beginning in November, the first news of her playing basketball did not appear in the local paper until January of 1938. In Wirt Gammons' sports column, "Just Between Us Fans" which appeared in the January 7 issue of the *Chattanooga Daily Times*, he reported, "Jackie Mitchell is playing with a girls' basketball team, booked out of Cleveland, O., and making a nation-wide tour."

The team that Jackie was playing for was a club called the Stars of the World, managed by former major league pitcher, Grover Cleveland Alexander. Mitchell and Alexander would have previously crossed paths back in 1933 when both were affiliated with the House of David baseball teams. Mitchell played for the Eastern club while Alexander managed the Central team.

There are no press reports about the launching of this new team, despite having both Alexander and Mitchell affiliated with it. There is also some doubt as to the team being "booked out of Cleveland." This is supported by a March 21, 1941, news story in the *Rhinelander (WI) Daily News*. The story detailed the travel basketball career of Helen Onson. According to the story, "Helen started out with Grover Cleveland Alexander's Stars of the World in January of 1938. The Stars had played a game in Rhinelander earlier that month. In response to a telegram, she joined them in Green Bay two days later. That was the year the great Grover was elected to Baseball's Hall of Fame in Cooperstown, N.Y. Grover also appeared with the New York Shamrocks, sponsored by the same Empire Hotel in Springfield, Illinois, which had the former pitcher on its payroll and which promoted the Stars of the World."

The Springfield connection would seem to be the logical base for the Stars team. Alexander had landed in Springfield in January of 1937 with a severe leg infection and with all of nine cents in his pockets, according to newspaper stories. Johnny "Buster" Connors, a veteran fight promoter and proprietor of the Empire Hotel, saw that Alexander was treated at the hospital for the infection. He later gave him a job as a greeter at the hotel and hired the former baseball star to manage Connors' semi-pro baseball club.

Although speculation, it is possible that Connors hired Alexander to manage the Stars of the World to bring his name back into the press. Alexander had just missed being voted into the Baseball Hall of Fame in 1937, and perhaps Connors surmised that the additional press for him might put him over the top for a 1938 selection. Connors had already brought the New York Shamrocks men's basketball team to train and be based out of Springfield, Illinois, for 1937-38 and possibly decided to create an all-female basketball club which Alexander would manage.

Of the original five players on the Stars roster, two players, sisters Delora "Ducky" Steele, 21, and Dessie Steele, 25, lived but a few miles from Springfield in Riverton, Illinois, and were well-known athletically. Dessie in particular, was a noted lefthanded pitcher, hurling for local teams from the time she was 17 years of age. Anita "Fern" Simmons, 21, and Isabel "Izzy" Payne, 26, both had played for women's basketball teams in Missouri and southern Illinois. Jackie Mitchell, 25, was the only one of the original five players who did not play basketball in or around the Springfield area. However, that prior House of David connection to Alexander and her time with Babe Didrikson's All-Americans might have been the draw to have her on the roster.

The Stars of the World opened their season on Christmas evening in Centralia, Illinois, against the DeMolays. In the first two minutes of the game, the DeMolays had scored 10 points according to the *Centralia Evening Sentinel*, in route to a 53-20 win over the Stars. The *Sentinel* went on to add, "In the fourth quarter it got to the place where the girls had their out-of-bounds passes from under the basket intercepted four out of five times and immediately converted into DeMolay goals." Guard "Izzy" Payne scored half of her teams 20 points and "looked like as though she had spent quite some time on a basketball floor," added the *Sentinel*. Jackie Mitchell started the game as a forward and scored two points. The news story did not mention if Alexander was with the club or not.

The next two games for the Stars were in Cynthiana and Berry, Kentucky. On December 25, the *Lexington Herald* (Kentucky) newspaper reported that a female basketball team called the Stars of The World, was scheduled to play in Cynthiana, Kentucky on December 28. The article was also the first to mention, "The girl's team is under the management of Grover Cleveland Alexander, formerly one of the greatest pitchers in the National League." The story went on to note, "Jackie Mitchell, one of the players, became famous as a baseball pitcher when she struck out Babe Ruth and Lou Gehrig." No results were listed for either game.

Following their slated games in Kentucky, the Stars would travel next into Michigan. Their first contest was against the Manistique All-Stars who were comprised of players from the local City Basketball League. With just their five players (Manistique would use 11), the Stars trailed by only two points after the first quarter and three points at half time. The Stars would lead their hosts 18-17 after the third quarter, but a late basket by Manistique would cause the Stars to fall by a score of 26-25. Four of the five Stars would score, including "Izzy" Payne and Fern Simmons, each tallying eight points. Jackie Mitchell was the lone member of the squad who failed to score.

Beginning on January 20, the Stars had three more Michigan games on their slate. Prior to their first scheduled game in Michigan, the Stars manager, Grover Cleveland Alexander was announced as the newest member of the Baseball Hall of Fame on January 19.

The first stop for the Stars was a game against the Ontonagon Pirates in Ironwood, Michigan, on the 20th, followed by a game against the Nahma Brews on the 21st, and the Rock Spartans on the 22nd. The lone published result from these three scheduled games was another one-point loss, this time to Nahma, by a score of 20-19. "Izzy" Payne again led the team in scoring with seven points. Missing from the line-up that game was Fern Simmons.

Two local players were picked up by the Stars, including a player with the last name of Robb and a former high school player by the name of Orla Ward. It would be the first time in the Stars season where they would have more than five rostered players. Robb would tally on point while Ward would score four points. "Ducky" Steel would score three points while sister Dessie would score two points. Mitchell would again be the lone member of the Stars not to score.

Following their games in Michigan, the Stars would head on to a series of games in Wisconsin, starting with a January 23 game against the Rhinelander Rhinos. According to the *Rhinelander Daily News*, the Stars had dropped the game by a 34-17 score but, "The gals could pop 'em in from a distance and they were all good shots, but naturally were no match for the rangy Rhinelander outfit. Playing without reserves, the gals were really bushed long before the timer would let 'em leave." A second game scheduled in Algoma was canceled due to snowy weather. A third game played in Neillsville, had the Stars come out on the short end of a 42-19 score.

Although news releases would proceed the arrival of the Stars as they went from town to town, the stories would mention Alexander and Mitchell most of the time as the two drawing cards. It wasn't until the end of January when more details would come out about the other team members.

One such news story appeared on January 27, in *The Daily Chronicle* from DeKalb, Illinois:

"Captain of the team is 'Izzy' Payne, reputed in the advance dope to be the world's greatest girl basketball player. She played with the high school at Greenwood, Missouri, and with Kirksville Teachers College in that state. For a time she was with the St. Louis All Stars and even played with a man's team.

" 'Ducky' Steele was born in Riverton and played early basketball with Springfield. She plays forward and is the best shot of the squad; is 25 years of age and also plays baseball.

"Youngest member of the team is 21, a sister of Ducky. Her name is Bessie Steele. She plays forward and is an excellent shot.

"Fern Simmons was born in Denver, Colo., played basketball with Shelbina High School in that state. Later she played with various clubs in Missouri, Kansas and Illinois. Is 22 years of age, plays center, and another good shot.

"Jackie Mitchell is from Chattanooga, Tenn., is 25 years of age, and has appeared in several movie newsreels. She is quite versatile. Was an orchestra leader in her hometown, flies an airplane, good swimmer, and the first girl ever to play in organized baseball."

Early February found the Stars making a trek into both Minnesota and Illinois. On February 2, they dropped a 48-30 game to a Grand Rapids team and two days later, the Stars came out on the short end of a 28-19 score against the Brainerd Bunyanites. In that game, Dessie Steele led the Stars with nine points, while "Izzy" Payne tallied four; "Ducky" Steele, Fern Simmons and Helen Onson each scored a basket. Jackie Mitchell was the lone Star not to make it into the scoring column.

On February 6, it appears that the Stars played an afternoon and evening basketball doubleheader. The first contest was in Sycamore, Illinois, against the Uptown team. While there was not a result for the game posted, *The Daily Chronicle* of DeKalb, stated that the game drew, "the largest crowd in several years to attend a non-scholastic game in Sycamore was rocking back and forth in a tornado of laughter." The article went on to add, "Miss Mitchell demonstrated with a baseball between the second and third quarters. With Cone catching, she pitched about a dozen over what should have been home plate. The pitches seemed to have a lot of zip behind them and fair control. She is the only girl pitcher in organized baseball today. She has pitched for the House of David team."

The evening tilt was played at the Coliseum in Rockford against the Thomist Friars. Before the start of the game, Alexander gave a brief talk to the 500 fans in attendance. Despite outscoring the Friars by a 12-8 margin in the fourth quarter, the Stars would drop the contest by a 33-26 margin. "Ducky" Steele led the Stars in scoring with 12 points while sister Dessie and "Izzy" Payne each tallied six points. Helen Onson added a basket, but Fern Simmons and Mitchell did not score.

After this basketball twin bill, the season for the Stars appeared to be over. On February 15, the *Daily Illinois State Journal* headline read: "Alexander Turns Cage Pilot, Will Tour West Coast." The story went on to say, "Grover Cleveland Alexander, who recently entered baseball's Hall of Fame as one of its greatest pitchers, has turned basketball manager and will lead a troupe of barnstorming hardwood artists on tour." The article went on to add that he would tour with the "New York Shamrocks" and be "an added attraction as the team tours the west coast, playing a series of games with Jesse Owens' Olympians, professional Colored quintet. Stated Alexander, 'I don't know much about managing a basketball team, but one never should be too old to learn'."

While the Stars waited to see if they would take to the court again, Alexander would spend two weeks in California and Arizona with the New York Shamrocks. The venture did not always run smoothly. News accounts mention that after arriving in California, the Shamrocks' bus turned up missing and a game played at the Civic Auditorium in San Francisco almost did not take place as the rental fee for the facility had not been paid. Auditorium management refused to open the doors until the bill was paid. After a delay of half an hour, it was agreed that the parties would share the first $100 to come into the box office. Overall, the monies collected that night would total $110 from the 25 fans in attendance. In order to play the game a fan was recruited to serve as a referee and the final score (depending on what newspaper you read) was either a 36-35 win by the Olympians (*San Francisco Chronicle*) or a 36-35 overtime win by the Shamrocks (*Oakland Tribune*).

A little more than a month after their last scheduled game, the Stars, again under the direction of Alexander, would again take to the court. On March 8, in Gordon, Nebraska, the Stars would battle the local town team, but would again drop their contest by a score of 44-30. The *Gordon Journal* reported, "The girls not only played by men's rules but played the game 'free style' with no holds barred." It went on to add, "The girl baseball pitcher who gave a pitching demonstration between the halves put on a fine exhibition which was greatly enjoyed."

The Stars of the World would end their one and only season with a documented record of 0-9, with five games either not played or no score reported. While the Steele sisters ("Ducky" and Dessie), Fern Simmons, "Izzy" Payne and Helen Onson would go on to play basketball during the next few seasons, that was not the case for Jackie Mitchell. The end of the Stars' season would be the final time that Mitchell would compete athletically in a sport. She would return to being a regular citizen of Chattanooga, out of the spotlight, except for periodic mentions of her 1931 strikeouts of Babe Ruth and Lou Gehrig.

CHAPTER 13
In Jackie's Voice

The voice of Jackie Mitchell has been silent since she passed away in 1987. After she retired from baseball in 1937 and during the last 47 years of her life, she was not interviewed extensively and in most of those interviews, they focused on the strikeout of Babe Ruth and Lou Gehrig.

This chapter has been created with Jackie's own words from interviews between 1931 and 1933 from newspapers all over the United States. The chapter will hopefully give a better insight to Jackie while she was an active player and not looking back years after retiring from baseball.

This is the most extensive list of Jackie's thoughts and comments that has been compiled. Many of these comments have not appeared in print for decades.

On signing her Lookout's contract ------- *This chance is an answer to a dream. I have made good.* (1931)

Baseball thoughts ------- *Maybe I am a bit odd, but somehow baseball has always been in my mind. Everything I've ever planned is in connect to baseball. I can pitch. I've proved that. I am no different that any other girl, except that I play baseball.* (1933)

There's nothing in the world I'd rather do than play baseball. (1933)

I've been a pro for three years, down south. Thousands have seen me. I think girls will have a chance in the big leagues some day. (1933)

Next spring I'm going back to Chattanooga and if I continue to improve maybe I'll get the chance. I know it doesn't look very likely, but you can't tell. (1933)

I guess I like to hit as well as anything. (1933)

How long have I played baseball? Well, I guess ever since I was two. Oh yes, I love to play baseball. Love to watch it too. (1931)

Everything I've ever planned however, is in connection with baseball. I've proved that. I've pitched winning baseball against Piedmont and Mid-Atlantic League Clubs. (1933)

Growing up ----- *I was born in Chattanooga and lived there all the time except for about three years in Memphis.* (1931)

Right and lefthanded ----- *I write with either hand and do everything except pitch about as well with the right as I do with the left.* (1933)

On facing Babe Ruth ------ *I did not know Babe Ruth had a weakness. I tried to outguess Ruth. The first one I threw was a ball, purposely high and close in, but the Babe would not strike at balls. The second one I pitched was a fast curve which broke in about waist high. Ruth swung and missed. The third ball I threw was a fast one in close about shoulder high. I have never had anyone hit this ball very far. Again he swung and missed. I though he would look for another one close in and high, so I threw the next one down the alley with all the smoke I could put on it. The Babe let this one go but the umpire called it for the third strike.* (1931)

He didn't say anything. Just threw the bat down and walked away. (1933)

On facing Lou Gehrig ----- *I threw three to Gehrig in close and a little above the waist line and he joined Ruth on the bench. I have always found most batters weak on this kind of ball.* (1931)

On Ruth & Gehrig ----- *I am glad of having had the pleasure of pitching against Mr. Ruth and Mr. Gehrig. I think they are both fine men and great ballplayers. I see nothing strange about my striking them out, at least stranger things have happened. Not even the best batters can hit them all. I only tried my best and I am the happiest girl in the world. I hope there may be other girls who will have the thrill of playing in organized baseball. I expect to pitch for years to come and shall try to get into a world series.* (1931)

On Lookouts manager Bert Neihoff ------ *I am sorry Mr Neihoff took me out. I still believe I might have won the game.*

On Eddie Kenna (her catcher on the Lookouts) ----- *Through the years of constant practice and coaching of Eddie Kenna, one of the greatest catchers of them all, I have gained, I think, wonderful control.* (1931)

Printed in the USA
CPSIA information can be obtained
at www.ICGtesting.com
LVHW012132121024
793675LV00007B/288

1930
Engelettes --- Chattanooga Girls Baseball League

DATE	OPPONENT	G	GS	CG	IP	H	R	BB	SO	W	L
6/7	Soddy Hosiery Mills	1	1	1	*	6	12	*	*	1	-
6/14	Peerless Woolen Mills	1	1	1	*	8	20	4*	10	-	1
6/21	Richmond Arrowheads	1	1	1	9	19	25	*	*	-	1
7/3	Bacon Hosiery Mills +	1	-	-	3	*	*	*	*	-	1
7/12	Richmond Arrowheads	1	1	*	*	*	*	*	*	-	1
7/19	Soddy Hosiery Mills	1	*	*	*	*	*	*	*	*	*
8/2	Richmond Arrowheads	1	1	1	*	*	19	*	10	1	-
8/9	Soddy Hosiery Mills	1	1	1	*	17	17	*	*	-	1
9/13	Buster Browns+	1	1	*	*	*	8	*	9	1	-
	League Totals*	7	6	5	9	50	93	4	20	2	4
	1930 Totals*	9	7	5	12	50	104	4	29	3	5

*Incomplete Boxscore Data

+Men's Team

1931
Chattanooga Lookouts

DATE	OPPONENT	G	GS	IP	H	R	BB	SO	W	L
4/2	New York Yankees #	1	-	2/3	0	0	1	2	-	-
	Totals	1	-	2/3	0	0	1	2	-	-

Exhibition game

1931
Junior Lookouts

DATE	OPPONENT	G	GS	IP	H	R	BB	SO	W	L
5/6	Alcoa (TN)	1	1	1	1	2	*	1	-	-
5/10	Penn Dixies	1	1	3	1	0	1	0	-	-
5/12	Tennessee Wesleyan	1	1	1	2	0	*	*	-	-
5/14	Rockwood (TN)	1	1	*	*	*	*	*	-	-
5/16	Dalton (GA) All Stars	1	1	1	4	3	*	*	-	1
5/17	Tennessee Products	1	1	2	1	3	*	*	-	-
5/24	Tullahoma (TN)	1	1	1	3	3	*	*	-	1

1931
Junior Lookouts (con't)

DATE	OPPONENT	G	GS	IP	H	R	BB	SO	W	L
5/28	Sewanee (TN)	1	1	*	2	1	*	*	-	-
5/30	New York Bloomer Girls **	1	1	3	0	0	*	*	-	-
5/31	Dyersburg (TN)	1	1	1	*	*	*	*	-	-
6/3	Athens (AL)	1	1	*	*	*	*	*	-	-
6/4	Florence Wilson Dam	1	1	2	2	0	*	1	-	-
6/5	Lincoln Mills	1	1	1	1	1	*	*	-	-
6/6	Southern Railway	1	1	*	*	*	*	*	-	-
6/7	Memphis Steam Laundry	1	1	2	5	5	*	1	-	-
6/7	Jolly Cab	1	-	1	2	2	*	*	-	1
6/10	Columbus Creamery (MS)	1	1	1	*	*	*	*	-	-

1931
Junior Lookouts (con't)

DATE	OPPONENT	G	GS	IP	H	R	BB	SO	W	L
6/12	L & N Shop	1	1	2	1	0	*	*	-	-
6/17	Cedartown	1	1	*	*	*	*	*	-	-
6/19	Lindale	1	1	2	*	6	*	*	-	-
6/20	Coca Cola	1	1	*	*	*	*	*	-	-
6/21	Lebanon	1	1	2	0	*	*	*	-	-
	Junior Lookout Totals *	22	21	25	25	26	1	3	-	3

*Incomplete Boxscore Data

**Women's Team

1931
Solo Appearances

DATE	TEAM	G	GS	IP	H	R	BB	SO	W	L
6/14	Lexington	1	1	3	2	1	1	*	-	-
6/26	Atlanta	1	1	3	*	4	*	*	-	-
7/15	Morristown Junior Order	1	1	2	2	3	*	*	-	-
7/18	Goodyear (Akron, OH)	1	1	2	*	0	*	1	-	-
7/19	Graney Nighthawks	1	1	2	1	0	*	1	-	-
7/29	Middlesboro (KY)	1	1	2	*	7	*	*	-	-
8/1	Morristown Junior Order	1	1	2	*	2	1	*	-	-
	Solo Game Totals *	7	7	16	5	17	2	2	-	-
	1931 Totals *	30	28	41.2	30	43	4	7	0	3

*Incomplete Boxscore Data

1932
Piedmont League

DATE	TEAM	G	GS	IP	H	R	BB	SO	W	L
8/13	Durham Bulls	1	1	2	*	*	*	*	-	-
8/16	Raleigh Caps	1	1	2	*	*	*	*	-	-
8/18	Charlotte Hornets	1	1	3	*	*	*	*	-	-
8/19	Greensboro Patriots	1	1	3	*	*	*	*	-	-
8/20	High Point Pointers	1	1	2	*	*	*	*	-	-
8/23	Greensboro Patriots	1	1	2	*	*	*	*	-	-
	TOTALS # *	6	6	14	*	*	*	*	-	-

All Piedmont Appearances Were Exhibition Only

*Incomplete Boxscore Data

1932
Solo Appearances

DATE	TEAM	G	GS	IP	H	R	BB	SO	W	L
8/25	Thomas Mills Tommies #	1	1	2	2	1	*	*	-	-
8/30	Martin Sales	1	1	3	2	1	0	0	-	-
9/4	Suffolk A.C.	1	1	3	4	2	*	*	-	-
9/5	Waddey	1	1	1.1	0	2	4	*	-	-
9/10	Norfolk Orioles	1	1	3	*	7	*	*	-	1
	EXHIBITION GAME TOTALS #	1	1	2	2	1	*	*	*	*
	GAME TOTALS	4	4	12.1	6	13	4	*	-	1

*Incomplete Boxscore
Exhibition game

1933
Regular Games/Exhibition Games

DATE	TEAM	G	GS	IP	H	R	BB	SO	W	L
5/28	Ironton	1	*	2	*	*	*	*	-	-
6/3	Beckley Black Knights (Middle Atlantic League) #	1	1	3	*	3	*	*	-	-
6/4	Welch Senators	1	1	3	1	*	*	*	-	-
6/25	Hopewell	1	1	3	*	3	1	*	-	-
7/2	Trenton Cadets	1	1	3	*	3	1	1	-	-
	Exhibition Totals *	1	1	3	*	3	*	*	-	-
	Game Totals *	4	3	11	1	6	1	1	-	-

#Exhibition game

*Incomplete Boxscore Data

1933
House of David

DATE	OPPONENT	G	GS	IP	H	R	BB	SO	W	L
7/17	Brown Hunter's Grays	1	1	1	*	*	*	*	-	-
7/18	Milton Bradley	1	1	1	2	1	1	-	-	-
7/19	Greenfield Mohawks	1	1	1	0	0	1	1	-	-
7/27	Wooster	1	1	1	*	0	*	*	-	-
7/27	Taunton Lumber	1	1	*	*	*	*	*	-	-
8/2	Mercury (VT)	1	1	1	1	0	0	0	-	-
8/4	Guy's Ball Club (NY)	1	1	1	2	2	2	-	-	-
8/6	Canton Pirates (NY)	1	-	1	0	0	0	0	-	-
8/7	Oswego	1	1	1	4	1	0	0	-	1
8/8	Byrne-Seiberlings	1	1	1	0	0	0	0	-	-
8/12	Elmira Redwings (NY)	1	1	1	4	3	*	*	-	-
8/15	Wilkes-Barre Barons	1	1	1	1	0	0	1	-	-
8/17	Huntingdon All Stars	1	1	1	0	0	1	0	-	-
8/18	Somerset (PA)	1	1	1	*	*	*	*	-	-

*Incomplete Boxscore Data

1933
House of David (con't)

DATE	OPPONENT	G	GS	IP	H	R	BB	SO	W	L
8/20	Zieglers (OH)	1	1	1	0	0	0	0	-	-
8/21	Westinghouse Electrics	1	1	1	3	3	0	0	-	-
8/22	Carey Semi-Pros	1	1	*	*	*	*	*	-	-
8/23	Skrzycki (MI)	1	1	2/3	0	1	1	0	-	-
8/24	Battle Creek Postums	1	1	1	-	0	-	-	-	-
8/27	Central House of David	1	-	2/3	0	0	0	1	-	-
9/4	St. Paul Saints	1	1	1	2	0	*	*	-	-
9/12	St. Louis Cardinals	1	1	1	1	0	0	0	-	-
9/22	Lacrosse (WI)Troubadours	1	1	1	3	2	0	1	-	-
	House of David Totals *	23	21	20.1	24	13	6	3	-	-
	Season Totals*	27	24	31.1	25	19	7	4	-	1

*Incomplete Boxscore Data

1934
Exhibition Games

DATE	Team	G	GS	IP	H	R	BB	SO	W	L
6/29	Xenia (Ohio) #	1	1	2	*	*	*	*	-	-
6/30	Columbus Redbirds #	1	1	2	*	*	*	*	-	-
7/3	Zanesville (Middle Atlantic League) #	1	1	2	*	*	*	*	-	-
7/18	Harrisburg (NY-Penn League) #	1	1	2	1	*	*	*	-	-
7/21	Reading (NY-Penn League) #	1	1	2	*	*	*	*	-	-
7/25	Hazleton (NY-Penn League) #	1	1	2	2	0	*	*	-	-
8/5	Elmhurst Grays #	1	1	2	4	4	0 @	2	-	-
8/14	Springfield (Northeastern League) #	1	1	1	*	*	*	*	-	-
9/15	Albany (International League) #	1	1	2	*	*	*	*	-	-
	Exhibition TOTALS #	9	9	17	7	4	0	2	-	-

*Incomplete Boxscore Data
@ ONE BATTER HIT BY PITCH

1934
Solo Appearances

DATE	TEAM	G	GS	IP	H	R	BB	SO	W	L
7/29	Jerseys	1	1	2	1	0	1	*	-	-
8/30	Brownies	1	1	2	2	0	*	2	-	-
9/3	Henricks	1	*	*	*	*	*	*	-	-
9/4	Copke's All Stars	1	-	1	*	*	*_	*	-	-
9/4	West Stockbridge	1	-	1	*	*	*	*	-	-
	TOTALS	5	2	6	3	0	1	2	-	-

*Incomplete Boxscore Data

1937
Buck Lai's Hawaiians

DATE	OPPONENT	G	GS	IP	H	R	BB	SO	W	L
6/13	Killian Celtics (Ohio)	1	1	1	2	0	-	-	-	-
6/21	Penn Drakes	1	1	1	2	0	0	1	-	-
6/23	Warren Independents	1	1	1	2	0	-	-	-	-
6/24	Hanley Bricks	1	1	1	0	0	0	1	-	-
6/28	Clearfield Indians*	1	1	1	0	0	0	0	-	-
6/29	Concordia Singers	1	1	1	*	0	-	-	-	-
7/3	West Shore All Stars	1	1	1	0	0	0	*	-	-
7/8	West York Firemen*	1	1	1	0	0	0	0	-	-
7/11	Bushwicks	1	1	1	0	0	0	2	-	-
7/16	Poughkeepsie All Stars	1	1	1	-	0	-	-	-	-
7/22	Savitt's Gem	1	1	1	-	-	-	-	-	-
7/23	Milton Bradley	1	1	1	-	-	-	-	-	-
7/27	Lowell All Stars* @	1	1	1	-	-	0 @	-	-	-

*Exhibition Game   @Two Batters Hit By Pitch

1937
Buck Lai's Hawaiians (con't)

DATE	OPPONENT	G	GS	IP	H	R	BB	SO	W	L
7/28	Norton Co.	1	1	1	*	*	*	*	-	-
8/2	Cobakco	1	1	1	*	*	*	*	-	-
8/3	Sayre Systems Shop #	1	1	1	*	*	*	*	-	-
8/5	Jamestown All Stars	1	1	1	1	0	*	*	-	-
8/10	Mansfield Red Sox (Ohio State League) #	1	1	1	*	*	*	*	-	-
8/18	Roosevelt Oil	1	1	1	0	0	*	1	-	-
	EXHIBITON GAME TOTALS	5	5	5	0	0	*@	1	-	-
	GAME TOTALS	14	14	14	7	0	0	5	-	-
	SEASON TOTALS *	19	19	19	7	0	0	6	-	-

*Incomplete Boxscore   @Two Batters Hit By Pitch
#Exhibition game

Career Totals*

Year	G	GS	CG	IP	H	R	BB	SO	HBP	W	L
1930	9	7	5	12	50	104	4	29	-	3	5
1931	30	28	0	41.2	30	43	4	7	-	0	3
1932	11	11	0	28.1	8	14	4	0	-	0	1
1933	28	25	0	34.1	25	22	7	4	-	0	1
1934	14	11	0	23	10	4	1	4	1	0	0
1937	19	19	0	19	7	0	0	6	2	0	0
TOTALS *	111	101	5	158.1	130	187	20	50	3	3	10

*Incomplete Boxscore Data

Myrion Pro and Britannic Bold on LSI 50# archival white
Type and Design by Karen Paul Stone
Charts by John M. Kovach

On fans ----- *I pitched scoreless for seven successive innings in a total of six games and then had a run scored on me. Some fans booed and said I wasn't so much. That hurt a lot because I, like every ballplayer, aim to please. But if I had pitched eight successive innings all on the same night and had not been scored upon until the eighth, when only one run would have counted, the fans would have taken their hats off to me.* (1933)

On being at home ------ *Whenever I can I go to the kitchen stove and cook meals for myself and dad. I am a capable cook, can make my own clothes and am looking forward to home life some day. I've passed up vaudeville offers because I don't like being out in front of people. You do not mind it playing baseball or basketball because you get so interested in the game, matching your skill and ability to think fast against someone else, that you forget there is anyone watching.*

Judge Landis ------ *I did well in the Southern League exhibitions until Judge Landis advised Joe Engel, Chattanooga Magnate, I couldn't play in league ball.* (1933)

House of David ------ *Touring with the House of David team is a fine experience. The players are wonderful in their attitude toward me and they are splendid, clean living athletes. But there is a hardship in the fact that the schedule makes me pitch at least one inning every day. I never did anything like that before. I used to pitch about once every five days. But now I have to go night after night.* (1933)

Too bad about the whiskers. Nature just didn't equip me for them. I'll be the only smooth-faced player in our club, won't I? But I can pitch. That's what counts. (1933)

They are an eccentric people, with a peculiar belief, but they are cultured and refined, as well as wealthy. (1933)

On her dad (Joseph S.) ----- *Dad gives credit to Vance; only once in awhile it is blame, not credit.* (1933)

On her mom (Virne) ----- *Mother doesn't like the idea at all. She cannot see baseball for a girl.* (1933)

On her sister Josephine ----- *Joe is a lot like Mother. She would not think of playing baseball. Tennis and swimming are her game, but she isn't enthusiastic over either of them. Her main hobby is drawing and painting. She wants to be an artist.* (1933)

Did Babe Really strikeout ----- *I'd rather he'd knocked it out of the park than to think he'd fanned out on purpose.* (1933)

Dazzy Vance ----- *My family were friends of Dazzy Vance, famous pitcher of the Brooklyn Robins. So I had the advantage of early instruction in the art of curves from this master.* (1931)

I was taught by Dazzy Vance when I was little. Yes, it was in Memphis. Yes, we lived in the same house with him then. (1931)

Staying in condition ----- *I manage to get nine hours of sleep every night. I retire early, eat a well balanced diet, including meats, vegetables, greens and fruits, never drink tea or coffee, let sweets and parties alone most of the time.* (1933)

Other Sports ----- *I played [basketball] with the Chattanooga Lookouts. The team is one of the best in the South.* (1933)

I have played basketball and done a lot of swimming. Baseball and swimming are my favorite sports. (1931)

What you do when traveling ----- *I do quite a bit of embroidery work and knitting. I visit the stores and shop around. I ride out with Dad to the parks and zoos. I visit universities and colleges.* (1933)

What will you use your baseball money for ----- *It is my intention to get to college and my contract with the Lookouts is a big financial help.* (1931)

After school ----- *Why, I think I will go on with baseball.* (1931)

CHAPTER 14
After Baseball

Following the end of the 1937 baseball season, Jackie Mitchell would play basketball for Grover Cleveland Alexander's Stars of the World team during the winter. That season ended in March of 1938, marking the last appearance by her in athletic competition.

During her first hiatus from the diamond in 1935-36, the shy Jackie generally stayed out of the spotlight. A rare exception was in the fall of 1935 when St. Louis Cardinals pitcher Dizzy Dean walked out of a benefit game in Chattanooga due to the lack of fans. Other than that instance, Jackie was content with being out of the public eye.

In 1936, her name was mentioned in many newspapers across the country. However, all were only marking that fifth anniversary of her appearance and strikeouts of Babe Ruth and Lou Gehrig.

By 1940, Jackie was settling back into life in Chattanooga. According to the 1940 census, both Jackie and her sister Josephine worked in their father's optometry business in Chattanooga. That same census showed both Jackie and her sister living with their mother Virne at 916 Oak Street.

In June of 1940, Jackie was part of a Ripley's "Believe It Or Not" sketch, noting that Jackie was the "First lady to sign a professional baseball contract and that she had struck out Babe Ruth and Lou Gehrig in succession in an exhibition game."

On September 6, 1941, the *Chattanooga Daily Times*, listed a number of locals who had been cited for reckless driving, including, "Miss Beatrice Mitchell who was living at 916 ½ Oak Street." Later that same year, on December 31, 1941, Jackie's mother would pass away.

During mid-April of 1943, the news from the ball diamond was front and center in Chattanooga. A lefthanded pitcher by the name of Mary Nesbitt has been recruited to sign with a new professional softball league that was being formed by Chicago Cub owner, Philip K. Wrigley, Jr. and Branch Rickey. The league became known as the All-American Girls Professional Baseball League (1943-54). Nesbitt was an outstanding softball pitcher in Florida, and her family moved to Chattanooga when she was ten years old. As she got older, there were no female softball teams – so she joined a men's team and pitched them to a city championship. That's where she caught the eye of the scouts from the new pro league, according to newspaper reports.

Nesbitt's signing would draw comparisons with Mitchell in the April 26, *Bristol News Bulletin* in Bristol Tennessee. "Mary is the second feminine left-hander here to achieve fame. The first was Lefty Jackie Mitchell who was signed by Joe Engel several years ago and pitched for the Lookouts in an exhibition game against the Yankees, striking out Babe Ruth and Lou Gehrig the fist time she faced the two great hitters."

For Mitchell, the announcement of a new professional women's league must have been bittersweet. However, a number of things would work against her joining. The league would be a hybrid between baseball and softball. Pitchers in the league would throw underhanded as in the softball circles. Mitchell, a baseball trained player, honed her skill in over-hand/sidearm deliveries. For the first three years of the league, pitchers would use the underhand delivery. Secondly, Mitchell would have been one of the older players had she entered. She would have been 30 years of age at the beginning of the 1943 season. Finally, Jackie had not been active in competitive athletics since 1938. That time off would have made it difficult to play at a high level.

On October 3, 1949, Jackie's father, Joseph S., would pass away in Oak Ridge, Tennessee, while visiting friends. Following his death, her father's will left Jackie a home at 2327 Fourth Avenue, while leaving his optical business and a home at 2506 Parkwood Avenue to his second wife, Frances. The remainder of Mitchell's estate was to be divided between Jackie and her sister Josephine, who was now living in Miami. On August 19, 1957, while visiting Jackie in Chattanooga, her lone sibling, Josephine, passed away at age 42.

When the Harrisburg Senators signed stenographer Eleanor Engle to play for their minor league team in 1952 (she never did play a game), stories about Jackie's signing again brought her briefly into the spotlight. In many of the stories, some of the facts comparing Engel's signing to Jackie Mitchell's were a bit hazy, given over 20 years had elapsed. *Nashville Banner* sportswriter Fred Russell tried to correct some misinformation about Jackie's 1931 appearance against the Yankees in his "Sidelines" column, "so that a factual account may be in order for those of us who weren't around twenty-one years ago." After recanting the strikeouts of Ruth and Gehrig, pitch by pitch that day, Russell ended his column this way: "Jackie was no super pitcher; she was just good…for a girl. But she is the only woman that ever struck out Babe Ruth, and at her home today, 3502 ½ Wilcox Boulevard in Chattanooga, she has the clippings and pictures to prove it."

On November 8, 1963, Jackie's name again appeared in the *Chattanooga Daily Times* as part of a community-wide list of individuals who had not voted in the previous four years and whose voter registration certificate was listed to be canceled.

According to the 1966 *Chattanooga City Directory*, both Jackie and Eugene A. Gilbert were employed by the Lerch's Red Bank Cleaners. Eugene was listed as a truck driver and Jackie was employed as a clerk. The very next year, the directory shows that the two had been married and were living at 835 Vine Street, (2nd Floor). Eugene was still employed as a truck driver for Lerch's while Jackie was working for Plymouth Lady as a checker. However, it appears that by 1972, the two were no longer together in the same household. In 1972, Jackie was still living at 835 Vine Street, but Eugene is not listed in the directory at all. In 1974, Jackie, employed by the Tidy-Didy Diaper Service, had moved, this time to 321 Dodson Avenue. Later that year, on November 1, Eugene Gilbert would pass away at age 68. Jackie would live at a number of different addresses in Chattanooga over the next few years, but by 1979, Jackie moved just across the state border to Fort Oglethorpe, Georgia.

Although fans would reach out to her via letters over the years, she still stayed well out of the public eye. A 1975 question from a writer in California to the *Chattanooga New Free-Press*, wondering "What had happened to Jackie Mitchell?" Sports editor Allan Morris asked the question in the newspaper and got a response from Jackie, herself – still living in Chattanooga! Consequently, Morris was then able to sit down to interview Jackie. It was probably the longest interview with her in nearly 40 years.

Morris had been at the April 2, 1931 game and saw Jackie fan Babe Ruth and Lou Gehrig.

Far removed from the spotlight of the 1930s, Jackie was retired and recently had suffered a broken ankle as well as undergone eye surgery. She was quick to share her scrapbooks and memories with Morris as well as commenting on the female athletes of today.

"Of course, we never heard of women's lib back then," said Jackie, "But I guess you could say that I was a pioneer in it." She went on to say, "I'm interested in keeping up with what's happening in female athletics and efforts of the girls to play against the boys. I think they ought to be allowed to, if they are good enough. There is one woman umpire in professional baseball now, and maybe someday there will be a player in the big leagues."

While Mitchell was happy to share her baseball memories with Morris, it was not long before she would again fade from the public eye. In 1981, the 50th anniversary of her strikeouts of Ruth and Gehrig were forgotten by the Lookouts.

In was in 1982, when a member of the Lookouts staff realized the oversight of the historic 1931 appearance by Jackie. Mitchell would be the special guest for 1982 Lookouts opening day. Prior to her appearance at Engel Stadium, local writer David Jenkins and photographer, Steve Grider ventured to Jackie's apartment located across from Lakeview-Fort Oglethorpe High School. There the two not only had the opportunity to visit with Jackie, but they also saw the scrapbooks from her career that had been started by her father. One had the article authored by Morris as one of its last entries.

That opening day appearance would re-energize the interest in Jackie and her strikeouts of Ruth and Gehrig. So much so, that when an individual in 1985 began to sell copied images from that historic day (not realizing that Mitchell was still living), a local attorney named Pam Berke stepped in to make sure that no one would take advantage of her.

A baseball fan to the end, Jackie was a diehard Atlanta Braves fan. Jackie would continue to live in Fort Oglethorpe, Georgia, until she passed away on January 7, 1987. Because of Berke's kindness to her, Jackie left her treasured scrapbooks to her friend.

Even in death however biographical information about Mitchell was still coming into question as both the Chattanooga newspapers, the *Times* and *News Free-Press* listed her as being a native of Falls River, Massachusetts.

On May 27, 2017, some 30 years after her death and over 75 years after her pitching appearance against the Yankees, the Chattanooga Lookouts honored her memory with a "Jackie Mitchell Bobblehead" which was given out to the first 1,000 fans that day.

It was a fitting tribute to Jackie Mitchell – the girl who loved baseball.

CHAPTER 15
Jackie By The Numbers

The following pages detail the pitching statistics of Jackie Mitchell's career. The statistics were gleaned from newspaper stories as well as box and line scores. In most cases, the game reporting was incomplete. However, this is the most complete record documenting the pitching appearances of Jackie Mitchell.

The most notable aspect of Jackie's pitching statistics are the number of games she starts and completes. In 1930 season with the Engelettes, she started seven games and completed five. The rest of her pitching career, she would be the starting pitcher in most of those (except for an occasional relief appearance). She would complete none of her starts, so statistically the complete game (CG) column will not be used after the 1930 season.

The boxscores for many of her games are not complete. Any category without a complete for a season, will list the available totals and an asterisk (*) to indicate when a record is not complete.

In seasons when Jackie is pitching exhibition games, they vary between one and three innings of work each time. As with the regulation games she pitched, these exhibitions are not counted as "wins" or "complete games", even though some newspaper reports credit her with winning the abbreviated pre-regular game exhibition. The statistics will merely document the fact that the exhibition appearance took place. It is interesting to note that of the only three batters that Jackie would hit in her seven seasons, all three were during exhibition games.

While other female pitchers before her, such as Lizzie Arlington, Maud Nelson and Alta Weiss would also have short stints as starters, they would also pitch far deeper into games and many times would complete them. In that respect, it becomes difficult to compare Jackie to other female pitchers. However, despite the lack on complete games in her record, there are aspects of her work that are noteworthy.

During her career, Jackie pitched for or against teams in at least eight different minor league circuits: Southern Association, Piedmont League, Middle Atlantic League, New York Penn League, Northeastern League, International League, American Association and Ohio State League. She also faced two major league teams, the New York Yankees and St. Louis Cardinals and managed not to surrender a run to either team.